EXPANDED EDITION

Windows

EXPANDED EDITION

JENNIFER JAMES, Ph.D.

 Newmarket Press • New York

87 88 89 90   10 9 8 7 6 5 4 3 2 1 HC
87 88 89 90   10 9 8 7 6 5 4 3 2 1 PB

The acknowledgments listed on page 146 constitute
an extension of this copyright page.

Library of Congress Cataloging-in-Publication Data
James, Jennifer, 1943–
    Windows.
    1. Conduct of life.   2. Spiritual life. I. Title.
BJ1581.2.J354   1987   081   87-24881
ISBN 1-55704-003-6
ISBN 1-55704-004-4 (pbk.)

Quantity Purchases
Companies, professional groups, clubs and other organizations may
qualify for special terms when ordering quantities of this title. For information contact: Special Sales Dept., Newmarket Press, 18 East 48th Street,
New York, New York 10017, or call (212) 832-3575.

Typography by Martin Type

Manufactured in the Unites States of America.

First Edition

For lecture or other book information, contact Jennifer James, Inc., 3903
East James, Seattle, Washington, 98122.

TO

Mom, Bob, David, Amy, Ken, Margo, Pat, Alene,
Charley, Robin, Cathy, Karen, Mary, Sylvia, Alice,
Roselle, Ginny, Laura, Kay, Joy, JoAnne, Carolyn, Dale,
Jack, Jan, Cindy, Sandi, Bertie, Diana, Georgianna,
Dan, Peter, Paula, Avis, Judith, Melodie, Joyce, Julie,
Tom, Kaye, Woesha, Racquel, Dorothy, Elizabeth, Don,
Sharon, Diane, Sarah, Jim, Jeanne, Leonard, Sandra,
Gene, Joan, Art, Chris, Rose, Anne, Charlene, Susan,
Sheila, John, Deanna, Shou, Sparkle, Carol, Jake, Julia,
Rafferty, Amanda, Jody, Karin, Lars, Janine, Michelle,
and the people of the Northwest

Love Comes in Simple Ways

EXPANDED EDITION

Preface

The word "perspective" turns up many times in this book. I know that my attitude, the way I see and think, is the most important element in my ability to feel good. Philosophers, counselors and writers tell us that perspective is a matter of choice.

A negative vision is like a grey filter turning everything into something less than it is and creating problems around every corner. ("We'll never find a parking place.") A positive attitude does the opposite. Things look as good as they can be and problems either go unnoticed or seem easy to resolve. ("It will work out fine.")

Optimists take risks because they believe anything is possible. Pessimists are afraid. Optimists bounce back; they have a built-in resilience. They talk and think about the future. Pessimists resist, fight and are diminished when faced with obstacles. They talk and think about the past.

Our view of reality is drawn from our culture, family patterns, education and life experience. It is deeply connected to our sense of personal value. We get what we expect. We get what we think we deserve.

I wanted more. I wanted to deepen my understanding of myself and my background. I decided that if I were responsible for my perspective, if I were making the choices, and if my perspective touched the quality of every moment of my life, I needed to enhance my ability to see what was really happening.

Trace back the ethnicities in your family. What are the biases and generalizations within your cultural patterns? What kind of community were you raised in? What did they tell you would happen to your life? One of the reasons we open up windows to the past through travel and researching our family history is to understand more about the mosaic we represent. You need to know.

Opening windows within yourself opens them externally as well. Opening windows in your history opens them into your future. Whatever our background, we now make the choices. Once I know how I see the world, I can opt to change it.

The first step for me was the "opening," the hit of light from an unexpected source. I call it a window. It is a glimpse of a better way to be. It is anything from where to put a cup-hook for convenience to a major philosophical shift: "I'd like to learn to forgive."

The windows push me to explore. I gather more information, read, talk to people and listen to my own heart. Gradually, the new possibilities connect within me. I hesitate, in limbo, tense about accepting a new, unfamiliar way. I feel as if I'm perched on a windowsill tipping out, then tipping back toward the comfort of a familiar room.

I push a little further, stretch towards the light and tumble through the opening to change. It's scary out there in space until I land, exhilarated, and feel the positive, wonderful energy, a change in my reality. "Why didn't I do this sooner?"

Then I want to share. "Listen to my new understandings!" Is there some way I can give this perspective—these incredible feelings—to others? Maybe I can, in bits and pieces, small openings into possibilities. Here they are.

When you are looking for questions or answers, join me. Dip into the unknown for supplies.

JENNIFER JAMES, Ph.D.
Seattle, 1987

*Each of us experiences life in our own context,
but for all of us there is a struggle to balance
the reality of life with our needs and our dreams.
Perhaps the most difficult thing of all is to value
our life and who we are, and to direct our life
in a manner that honors it . . .*

—LAURI HARPER
A Taste for Life

WINDOWS

When the present seems hopelessly bogged down, I turn, for a few moments, to the future.

I feel an intuitive attraction pulling me. I can see and feel the future. I know where we will travel if we move beyond our current life-patterns.

Crises always precede perceptual transformation. It's as if we need to be bumped into an ability to see clearly.

The choices seem obvious, but you must make the commitment.

connection, not elitism
empowerment, not power over others
community, not isolation
participation, not observation
self-discipline, not letting go
touching, not sex
intuition as well as logic
humor, not hopelessness
grace, not control
optimism, not pessimism
meaning as well as comfort
spirit, not emptiness

Open the window of the future that is within you. Peek out, stretch, lean toward it, and prepare to tumble through.

Reprinted from *Success is the Quality of Your Journey.*

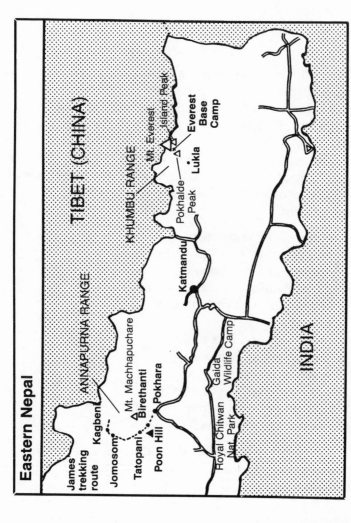

"The path I travelled on..."

SIGNPOSTS

Ch'ien/The Creative: When an individual draws this oracle, it means that success will come to him from the primal depths of the universe; and that everything depends upon his seeking his happiness, and that of others, in one way only, that is, by perserverance in what is good.
—I CHING

This is the day to think about rebirth, the new year. For me it will be a year of travel, to China, Tibet and elsewhere. It will be a year to travel within and without, a journey toward the heart.

I sometimes call it "trekking in the Inner Cosmos," to lighten my mood and lessen my own vulnerability. When we trek about in the depths of inner geography, gentleness and grace are only moments away from anger and pain.

When I started trying to understand, years ago, I chose anthropology as one path. I wanted to learn the answers cultures other than my own had chosen. I taught comparative religion, the universal search for ecstasy. I taught cross-cultural morals and values, the search for what is right. What I learned was respect for the God within all living things.

The journey continues. Take a few steps with me in honor of the new year. Choose your own way, listen to your own voices. Pick up guides wherever you can, but remember to let go of them so you can keep moving. Remember to take time to rest, now and then, to renew your spirit.

Start the new year with your own journey toward the heart. Here are some signposts to light your way. As you travel, remember that we are all connected, and that the destination is the same for all of us.

The longest journey begins with a small step and ends with a small step.—Anonymous. Take a step. If you don't like the step you chose, then try another until you find the one that is right for you.

I am lovable and capable. Sometimes others remind us that we are worthwhile people. Knowing you are worthwhile from within, mistakes and all, is the best daily reminder.

Self-knowledge is for the purpose of contributing. —Alene Moris. Take time to understand yourself. Self-knowledge is essential if you are to have a quality life.

You are the only one who can take care of your inner child. Are you still looking for the perfect mother or father? Are you still trying to improve the ones you have? Practice taking care of the child within you. Only you can do it right.

Happiness requires action. Happiness requires involvement, interest, commitment and a belief in meaning to our lives beyond ourselves.

Don't confuse kindness with weakness. Gentle people have special strength. Sometimes in others there is only an illusion of strength. Remember this in passion and love.

I am never upset for the reason I think. Check and see if you are afraid of something or angry for some other reason than what you started with.

If I hurt enough, I'll change. Pain is a wonderful and terrible teacher. If you feel tension, confusion, boredom or depression, your body is asking you to change.

Every problem has a gift for you in its hands.—Richard Bach. Wisdom comes from tapping our deepest emotions. It's learned by moving through problems, not by standing still. Use troubles to fine-tune your character.

I cannot control the thoughts and acts of others. Peace of mind requires you to realize you have no control over others. You may want someone to be more thoughtful, but you can't make him so.

All you need lies within. Self-knowledge is sometimes painful and very hard to find. When you do discover something about yourself, it's a wonderful accomplishment.

Love is something you do. Put love into the world and it will come back to you.

Angels can fly because they take themselves lightly. —*Jean Cocteau.* Try to see the absurdity in life. You deserve to laugh.

This, too, will pass. Time is a healing force. All painful things in our past become easier to handle with its passing. Feelings don't last forever unless you want them to.

I did the best I could with who I was and what I knew at the time. It is hardest to forgive yourself, even for things that happened long ago. If something is bothering you, make up for it in whatever way is left. Then let it go.

If you want inner peace you must give up inner conflict. It's easy to think that conflict (anger, fear, irritation) comes from what someone else is doing to us. Choose to react not with anger but with a positive peaceful thought.

What is not love is always fear.—*Gerald Jampolsky.* There are two basic emotions: all the things that feel like love, and everything else. Anger, arrogance, pride and depression are based on fear. List your fears. Then work on letting them go.

I could see peace instead of this. You can change your perception. Look for the positive hidden in every negative. Choose peace.

Enlightenment is being able to go to your own home and feel comfortable. Happiness comes from the inside, not the outside. Remind yourself of what brings you joy and peace. Set a goal to bring more of these things into your life.

Very few things are truly important. You may be expending energy repeatedly for things that are not truly important to you or your community. Ask yourself over and over again, "What is truly important?"

Success is the quality of your journey, not a destination. Success is every moment of your life—the quality of your interaction with living things. Choose quality whenever you can.

SUCCESS

People we admire as having successful lives have similar traits:

- They have a purpose in life beyond themselves.
- They set goals and make plans.
- They envision their plans being successful.
- They don't get trapped on a comfortable "plateau" very long.
- They solve problems, rather than blaming.
- They are optimistic and good-humored.
- They are concerned with quality, not just quantity.
- They understand they are in control.

All these traits are learned, not innate.

The definitions of "success" and "quality of life" are yours alone.

Only you determine what brings to each day joy, energy, passion and peace.

TODAY

"Love all of life. Each year brings its own pleasures—and sings its own songs."

—FLAVIA

There is always the temptation to live in the past or the future. "Well, things will be better tomorrow." "I'll enjoy life more when the sun is out." "I never enjoy Mondays." "I prefer June to March." "Things were better last year." "I'll be glad when this day, week, month or year is over."

It is possible with these thoughts to postpone your entire life waiting for the right moment.

We do it in work and relationships, too. "Oh, well, I'll put in a good day tomorrow." "I can be nice to her next time."

This is the moment. Stop and put some joy, some quality, some awareness into it now; a smile, a squeeze, a sip, a smell, or just take a deep breath. Cherish *your* life and hear the notes of each song. Up the scale or down, the music is always there.

SLOW DOWN

I lost some good friends last year. A few died. I lost touch with some others who lived at too fast a pace and closed the year sick or depressed. It's time to slow down, not just to protect your health and relationships, but so you can see and feel more clearly.

There was a time when I felt I had to rush through life. Nothing could stop me. Ecstasy was a day when I got 25 errands accomplished, caught no red lights, found the right parking space and no other customers got in my way.

I've been learning this lesson for years, but this Christmas "the spirit" kept eluding me. I finally realized the Christmas spirit travels at five miles per hour and I was traveling at 50. No time to hear music, smell pine boughs, or feel anything.

There will always be many good, important things to do, but life is better measured by quality, not quantity.

The new year is a time to decide again what is truly important. Take good care of yourself so next year you will not have lost friends or yourself.

I'll do it if you will.

BLISS

I was lucky enough recently to spend a few hours with Tom Robbins, the author of *Even Cowgirls Get the Blues* and other books. He reminded me to check my sources of bliss.

Go back to when you were a child and think about what made you happiest. Tom remembered giving dramatic readings to an audience of trees. He's still telling his stories to the world, and now he's letting us share them.

I remembered the iridescent beauty of the dragonflies on Newman Lake outside Spokane and the bleeding-heart bush by our front door. I've planted more bleeding hearts in my own yard, and am waiting for the dragonflies to visit my pond; they did last summer.

What are your sources of bliss? They are so simple, and yet many of us have lost touch. Close your eyes, take a deep breath and let the child within you smile.

PERSISTENCE

Improving our lives or environment always seems to cost more than we imagine. Making dreams come true requires hard work, risk, lots of doubt and times when we want to quit.

Remodeling a personality in some ways compares to working on a house. You never really finish. There are surprises behind the walls, and a feeling of disorientation when things are out of order, when patterns change. It's also easy for the neighbors to see what a mess you're in.

Sometimes all you're left with is your persistence. If you believe in yourself and want something enough, you keep working. On those cold, foggy mornings when you begin to question yourself or your latest project, remember why you're doing what you're doing. Remind yourself of your dreams, warm up your thoughts, and put one foot in front of the other.

SOLITUDE

My passionate interest in social justice and social responsibility has always stood in curious contrast to a marked lack of desire for direct association with men and women. I am a horse for single harness, not cut out for tandem or team work. I have never belonged wholeheartedly to country or state, to my circle of friends, or even to my own family. These ties have always been accompanied by a vague aloofness, and the wish to withdraw into myself increases with the years.

Such isolation is sometimes bitter, but I do not regret being cut off from the understanding and sympathy of other men. I lose something by it, to be sure, but I am compensated for it in being rendered independent of the customs, opinions, and prejudices of others, and am not tempted to rest my peace of mind upon such shifting foundations.

—ALBERT EINSTEIN

MOUNTAINS

I'm on another journey, struggling up some mountain in Nepal. My hikes are often the same. The journey toward the heart, the God within us.

Journey with me a little way up the mountain. Close your eyes, breathe the cool air, feel the solitude, step into another part of the spiritual world with me.

I'll do the puffing up the hill, and you can do the sharing of the spiritual load.

Every page while I climb, take a step yourself on your own spiritual journey. The journey toward the heart is always a journey home.

NEPAL JOURNEY I

I'm about to embark on a five-week journey, three of those weeks to be spent hiking about 110 miles through the mountains of Nepal.

It was difficult to sleep last night. Why wasn't I satisfied with something simple like going to Maui to lie in the sun? Why a trip to Katmandu and beyond?

As I'm bouncing around in my head I remember a friend telling me to measure the moments of life I had left. She calls it "learning to be mortal." Make sure you know what you want because there's only so much time. Life is precious. I am proud—if scared—to be an adventurer.

Packing, savoring the moments of anticipation, squeezing my new down vest, running my fingers through hair cut short for the trek and choosing books worth carrying in my backpack. Peter Matthiessen's *The Snow Leopard, Zen and the Art of Motorcycle Maintenance* by Robert Pirsig, and *Between Ourselves: Letters Between Mothers and Daughters*, edited by Karen Payne.

It's time to go, warming to my husband's support of my last-minute jitters, his openness to my travels. Enjoying the company of my son, David, as he drives me around on last-minute errands. Then, at the airport, David gives me a wonderful hug! We're not self-conscious anymore, now that my head barely reaches his chin.

Ecstasy—I'm on the plane and there's an empty row, so I can stretch out for the long flight. Flying makes me feel like a bird in its nest waiting to be fed. It's cozy, but I wish I could fly under my own power.

Looking around the plane I'm reminded how varied the world is. Passengers on the Seattle-Bangkok-Katmandu flight represent all colors, clothing styles and walks of life. Businessmen from Hong Kong, tourists from New Delhi, adventurers from everywhere. Somehow I'm one of them.

VALENTINES

"There is no such thing as love, only acts of love."

—Picasso

Love is supposed to feel good. Yet many of us get caught thinking love hurts. Not being loved hurts. Someone will say "I love you" while squeezing the knee of your best friend.

People will say "I love you," and then not come home at night. "I love you," says the parent who is hitting the child. "This is for your own good," says the person handing us a slug. "I wouldn't do this if I didn't love you." Help! With all that love, we could end up depressed.

You can give love to yourself—I hope you will—only by acts of love and kindness. You can love others the same way.

Let us join together and sidestep the talk, the promises, the illusion of love and go all out for the real thing, the acts of love.

Love is something you do.

RESENTMENT

Some African tribes believe forgiveness is essential to life. When a person falls ill, the relatives search for someone who harbors ill will. They assume a member of the family or tribe is holding onto resentments and causing the sickness, and that the patient will die if not forgiven.

The reverse is also true when we hold resentment inside. When we cannot forgive, we deny ourselves health and our future because we remain stuck in the past.

There are those who say we must never forget history or personal attacks because we will not remember to protect ourselves in the future. Pain is an incredible teacher; but we can learn and then let it go.

Forgive whenever you can. Work at it. Let go of guilt and resentment as tools of negotiation.

Your health, your survival and your peace of mind depend on your willingness to commit to tomorrow.

REST

It's time to relax. Put down all those lists, slow down your heartbeat, light a fire. Let the quiet soothe the productive beast within you.

Take the whole day to relax and review your feelings, values and priorities. It doesn't mean you'll get behind. You'll get to see ahead.

Draw some sustenance into yourself—deep breaths, solitude and peace.

You are much more than the sum of what you produce.

THE CALL

Throughout your life, there is a voice only you can hear. A voice which mythologists label "the call." A call to the value of your own life. The choice of risk and individiual bliss over the known and secure.

You may choose not to hear your spirit. You may prefer to build a life within the compound, to avoid risk. It is possible to find happiness within a familiar box, a life of comfort and control.

Or, you may choose to be open to new experiences, to leave the limits of your conditioning, to hear the call. Then you must act.

If you never hear it perhaps nothing is lost. If you hear it and ignore it, your life is lost.

DEALING WITH LONELINESS

Loneliness is a part of everyone's life, whether you live alone or not. It is a feeling of separateness. It is the human condition to be aware, to be internally separate. When you've felt alone too long, remember to:

- Move deeper within yourself
- Stretch your creative side
- Accept your spiritual connections
- Treat yourself as you would a lover
- Surround yourself with life in all its forms
- Connect yourself to the world by giving

One of the gifts of being human is the wisdom we gather within. It's a feeling we can draw from for all eternity.

SPRING

"All we do our whole lives is go from one little piece of holy ground to another."

—J.D. SALINGER

I feel anticipation everywhere. It's time to wander in the garden and breathe in all the new energy of spring. I'm always amazed at what lies just underneath the surface of our world.

It's time to shrug off the greyness. Time to swell inside like the buds on the flowering plum. Time to feel the peace within, the balance around us.

Time to stop for the moments of pleasure and know they are for you.

TIME

"Love brings much more happiness than efficiency."
—KEN KEYES, JR.
Handbook to Higher Consciousness

High tech and multiple options surround us; communication at ever-increasing speed and complexity. As our world changes faster, we move and think faster. Help! There is more to life than increasing its speed.

Happiness lies not in interaction with inanimate objects, but in deep connection with life (people, animals, plants), especially your own.

Pleasure is all around if you can see, hear, smell and feel it. The lament that "there's not enough time" is a signal to slow down and make contact. There is always just the right amount of time.

You can speed up your life if you want to—that's easy. Winding down is what's hard. Let go of the surface maintenance, dig a little deeper, take time to love.

SPACESHIP

This is a test! Turn your frequency to your best self and prepare for the future.

A spaceship lands in your front yard. *Hummmmm, lights flashing, whirr, thunk!* A door opens in the ship and a ramp descends to your feet. A bright light appears in the doorway and an arm beckons you up the ramp.

Are you going?

Are you going to wait and see what happens to your neighbor when he walks up before you decide?

Are you going to call the national guard?

End of test—did you pass?

What would a group of third graders have done? Up the ramp, fast—wow!

What's the difference between you and a third grader?

Experience? How much experience have you had with spaceships?

Perception?

You think any alien is after your stuff or your body—they think it's "E.T."

Steven Speilberg has given an entire generation of American children back the universe.

They're not afraid and we still are.

We see "alien," they see "friend."

It's time to open yourself to the world and the universe so you'll be ready when the invitation comes.

An invitation to be part of tomorrow.

BURDENS

Two monks were walking along the road, and came to a river. On the bank of the river was a beautiful young woman afraid to cross the river by herself. One of the monks gallantly stepped forth and offered her a ride on his shoulders. Upon reaching the other side, she thanked the monk, and they went their separate ways.

About one hundred steps down the road, the second monk said to the first, "How could you do that? You are a monk, a renunciate. You should not be carrying beautiful women around on your shoulders."

To which the first monk replied, "Oh, are you still carrying her? I let her down when we reached the shore."

TRADITIONAL ZEN STORY

What are you still carrying around? Who are you carrying it for?

ANOTHER CHANCE

The crocuses are up, the primroses are out and spring fever isn't far behind.

It's a great time of year because everything starts growing. Everything gets a second chance to bloom.

You do, too.

- Plant something to prove your optimism.

- Bring some branches in so the buds open early.

- Clean something, so it's fresh.

- Take a spring walk.

- Say "hello" to a neighbor; hibernation's over.

- Wake up earlier, with the light.

- Buy a bright spring sweatshirt.

This is it: time to stretch your body and mind, develop a few new shoots and check your buds.

CONTROL

Frustration, irritation, impatience, anger—the desire for control. We learn as children a terror of being at the mercy of events, situations and circumstances we cannot control.

Children of alcoholics and abusive parents have it burned into their soul.

The unpredictable grab or slap. The thrown glass that becomes a hurricane.

You want it to be different for you. But no matter how you try, how thoughtful you are, you cannot control the spouse, kids, dogs, friends. You seeth with fear and frustration. One snip of the taut wire and it will all come apart and you'll be a child again—caught.

You dream of a place for everything and everything in its place.

The fundamental mistake we make is in holding the belief that we have a responsibility to bring order into life. Everyone has a different sense of what that order should be. We assume because of our chaos that order is not natural; that disorder will occur if we do not impose on it. Slowly we realize that no amount of imposed order brings the control we hunger for.

Let go a little, of just one corner or drawer, relax, stop trying to impose your order on the world. Give up the illusion that it's essential for your safety.

Shift a little each day away from your fear of chaos and towards acceptance of the natural harmony around you.

PATCHES

The most beautiful people I have known are those who have known defeat, known suffering, known struggle, known loss, and have found their way out of the depths. These people have an appreciation, a sensitivity, and an understanding of life that fills them with compassion, gentleness, and a deep loving concern.

Beautiful people do not just happen.

—HISTORIAN ROY NICHOLS

Pain is a great teacher, but most of us would rather learn some other way. We think that happiness comes from a perfect childhood and avoiding mistakes. We don't like that patched-up feeling that comes with each survival. We would like to be seamless, no patches, no scars. Cherish your hard-won depth and understanding. Some pain is required for the journey. The gifts you seek are often disguised as problems.

Patches bring strength, whether on our knees or in our hearts.

OPTIMISM

I often write about optimism. It is part of the change happening in our culture. It is an essential characteristic for peace. For too long we confused pessimism with intelligence. Pessimism is inherited from pessimistic adults; it is a form of depression that sees a negative past and no future.

Check your outlook.

You make the choice: You can be a serious—"I must be intelligent"—intense, miserable pessimist who's probably depressed.

You can be a lighthearted, philosophical optimist who may be perceived as less aware and intelligent, but who is happy and at peace. Who has more to offer? Who may be more aware?

There is no way to feel fully alive unless you are willing to start your day with at least one optimistic option.

BEING

There is a subtle shift going on in our culture. We are changing from the "having" to the "being" mode.

The 1960s were a time of breaking loose because of the safety of our material foundation.

The 1970s were a time of introspection; we turned inward to check our values and ourselves.

The 1980s are a time to move toward being. It's time to overcome the myth of separation and material satisfaction.

Edward Lindeman, in his book *Thinking in the Future Tense*, reminds us that material goods are basic to human existence, but they are not the source of joy or richness.

Joy is found in creativity, personal relationships, quality, peace, culture, the human spirit and connection with living things.

Check your sources of joy.

JUSTICE

It's hard to forgive when you feel you are under attack. The desire for justice can easily shift to a desire for revenge.

When you're in a situation that feels like an attack, try to understand why.

What pain is the other person acting out? Try to spend a moment seeing from their perspective.

Anger is always fear. Can you let go of your fear?

Can you accommodate their need, or is it endless?

Can you let go even if they cannot?

You can choose to forgive while protecting yourself. You can choose peace while facing conflict. You can offer love when facing anger. Or you can wait for justice, as long as you remember:

Justice is much harder to find than peace.

FUTURES

Perhaps because it's spring, or maybe it's the influence of all the books and articles I read on the subject—the future is often on my mind.

Decide on your preferred future. Imagine it. Design it. Then work backward toward the present.

Check your visions: What do you want to happen?

Scout the terrain: What's already happening?

Imagine other possibilities: Invent your own hopes.

Make a commitment: Give power to the direction in which you decide to move.

What you imagine of the future determines what it will be. Quick! It starts now.

SABBATICAL

It's time for you to take a sabbatical.

There are many theories about our need for a change of pace and environment: a respite, a chance to think, a challenge.

Sometimes we wait for illness or burnout to force us to take a breath, but it's easier to just choose to slow down, look a little deeper, take a personal Chautauqua.

The ingredients are basic: solitude, time, a physical or intellectual challenge, nature and a step outside the limits of our own culture.

The first sabbatical I took was to Grenada, when it was an unknown, sleepy island. I stayed six weeks and replenished my body and soul. I was suffering then from too much growth too fast.

Now it's the opposite. I've been too busy to stretch in some of the ways I need. This time I'm going to try mountains to pull me up and onward to the next turn in the path.

It's time for you to put more passion into your life. Join me on my Nepal journey, plan your own sabbatical, and then travel with me to the mountains.

SIMPLE

It's camping season, the annual return to the woods.

The best style is as simple as possible: bread cooked in the coals, fish caught from the stream.

We need a reminder of the basics of life.

Camping gives us pleasure because of the profound simplicity of living without technology—the pleasure of concentrating on direct, life-related work. No multiple-option tension here. Just the single option of catching and cooking, slow conversation, marveling at caterpillars and tree sap, sleeping at dusk, waking at dawn.

Simple, peaceful, a respite in a world addicted to speed and complexity.

Your body tingles when you remember the woods are always waiting—ready to restore your perspective by reminding you of what you really need to be happy: clean air, quiet, the natural environment and a rainbow you caught yourself.

LET'S TALK

People keep calling us to our best selves.

They want us to take care of our bodies and our minds. They remind us that we are mortal, and we still think in terms of forever.

Then the elbow creaks and the wrinkles multiply.

It's time to hold a meeting.

Sit down and hold a meeting with your body: Imagine 6,000 cells, each with human features and each wearing a sweatshirt. Now explain to the liver cells why you are drinking things that make them sick. They want to know why they have to wear brown sweatshirts when they prefer red.

Talk to the cells in your lungs and explain why they cannot get their shirts clean. Explain to the stomach guys whey they need ladders to avoid the fat that's floating around them.

Try to convince the muscle and tendon team that they should jump whenever you ring the bell, even if it's only once a month. They refuse to even dress.

Last but not least, after checking in with all your other cell mates, what about the sex cells? They are promised romance, but they are getting either no action at all or no time to prepare their act.

True, this will be a long and difficult meeting, but they have been waiting a long time for you to show interest.

Negotiate, or prepare for a strike.

CREDIT

Getting attention is an essential survival mechanism for a baby. If adults don't notice the baby crying, it could starve. Getting attention also is essential for small children.

Many of us cannot shift from that small-child desire—to be noticed and given credit—to the adult system of internal credit.

Test yourself; can you share credit? Try giving credit to someone else which you might have kept for yourself.

How do you feel when no one notices your contribution?

Start measuring yourself by your personal value system.

You can get a lot more done if you don't care who gets the credit.

MALENESS

Women have asked, "When will men find themselves as women have?" Robert Bly has answered: *"Men are finding that their strength lies not only in their newly acquired female sensitivities but in their deep masculine self."*

In their desire not to abuse the physical power of their maleness, some men have hesitated to show it. They have lost touch with their own depth and strength.

Don't confuse kindness with weakness. Don't confuse your energy force with violence. Stay in contact with your heart.

SOMETHING MORE

"I am sure there is something more."

"If only I could meet the right man or woman."

There is something more. The feeling of belonging to a family, a love for your brothers and sisters that has nothing to do with couples.

The family is the human one. The love is shown through concern for the future and for those who are at risk. That love is at least as valid and rewarding as the love we try to give to just one person.

We get lost in loneliness looking for a single mate when there is a whole world waiting. The impulse to mate is powerful, but there is a shift taking place on our planet, a shift toward connecting with the spirit in others, a shift away from couples in little boxes.

"There is no enterprise which is started with such tremendous hopes and expectations and which fails so regularly as romantic love."
—ERICH FROMM

There is no love that rewards with more consistency and provides lifelong passion as the love one has for the world.

PY

I spent an afternoon with Py Bateman last week. She gave me a powerful gift: the belief that I could fight for my life if I had to, and the determination to do it.

Py is the director of Alternatives to Fear. She has spent 14 years teaching women to protect themselves from sexual violence. Py has always believed intensely in what she was doing, even when her sisters sometimes doubted.

A few weeks ago, on a sunny afternoon, Py was brutally attacked outside her home. She was cut up, beaten, and ended up in critical condition, but she fought off her attacker. She cut her hands deeply pulling the knife away from her throat. She told me that throughout the long attack (they fought all over her house) she was determined to hold on, to keep control of herself. She cannot remember when it stopped and she lapsed into unconsciousness.

We sat across the table from each other, Py with her hospital haircut, scars from brain surgery, scars around her eyes from the knife, scars on her hands. She told me that she was planning to work even harder to teach women to conquer their fear. She knew it might save their lives.

Sitting with Py I felt afraid. I felt a new determination. I felt loved.

MORTALITY

I am learning to be mortal.

For such a long time I felt age or death could not touch me. Yet, I've been thinking about my older friends. We're putting a bathroom on our first floor, so they can visit without the indignity of being carried upstairs.

We still design our homes and lives as if we will live forever. Learning to be mortal requires that you take much better care of yourself and your friends.

Time then becomes an ally to cherish and enjoy, not an enemy always speeding ahead.

Keep your connections with older generations strong. They will share the wisdom and humor of time, remind you of your own mortality, and encourage you to live deeply and well.

OLYMPICS

The Olympics are wonderful. For a moment in time, fixed on the glowing faces of athletes and artists, anything seems possible.

We believe again in hard work, courage and reward. We believe again that nations have more in common than in conflict.

Olympic athletes have learned that both body and mind must work together. They have learned to visualize their goals.

The values are clear, the imperfections tolerable. The ethic survives: winning is still not as important as how you play the game.

How about an Olympics of the heart? A competition for clarity, centeredness and peace?

Anyone ready to carry the torch to thread families, states and nations together? Hard work, courage and the ability to see the goal are all it takes. Start with your own team. Stretch the muscles of your mind and heart.

We'll cheer you on. But only you will know if you've got the gold.

INTIMACY

The desire for intimacy with another human being seems as strong as life itself: it's the desire to escape the isolation, the aloneness of our human uniqueness. We confuse this desire so often with the sexual impulse that we often no longer understand what we want.

"Sex can be and often is specialized and standardized. Love is always unique, one of a kind.
"Sex strives for reliability and predictability. Love is eternally surprising."

—GEORGE LEONARD

Intimacy requires commitment on a deeply personal level; an affirmation of life, a commitment to know ourselves and to know another. The rewards are great: tenderness, exaltation, transformation. Leonard calls such commitment "high monogamy." It is the opposite of sex as exercise.

We all seek ecstasy, but fear leads us to sabotage our own joy—the joy in our ability to love, to create, to feel deeply.

TRUST

I want to help create more trust.

We don't trust each other enough. We are afraid of steps toward common values. We think we will be controlled, not enhanced, if we agree on certain things together.

It took us a long time to trust our society enough to invade individual freedom and begin to put pressure on drunken drivers. Now we are beginning to trust that we won't use a breathalyzer to hurt, but to prevent hurt.

It's taking us a long time to understand that we won't voraciously invade family privacy if we try to help abused children.

We're just beginning to feel we might stop molesters by taking away their access to children, and that this does not represent a loss of freedom, but a gain for freedom of children.

We're stuck when it comes to violent and child-pornography. Some librarians say if we remove one magazine, we will want to remove them all. Why do we have so little faith in ourselves? Why is it considered impossible to balance freedom with limits on displays of violence toward women and children?

I trust myself, I trust you, I trust our basic values and our deliberative process. It's time to take care of one another, it's safe to take care of one another, it's possible to take care of one another.

DREAMS

There are all sorts of dreams floating by.

Dreams are an essential part of our creativity, as long as we make them a real part of our life.

If you dream of having a better job, writing the great American novel, being svelte, or building a greenhouse, the question is: what step, however small, have you taken toward that vision?

If you dream of a genie who pops out of the bottle and cleans the whole house, why not clean out just one drawer yourself?

Lottery dreams are of security, independent wealth, new cars, trips around the world, gifts to those you love. What can *you* do while you wait for that winning ticket?

Pipe dreams occur when you don't trust your own dreams, and instead use alcohol or some other drug to squelch or alter your visions. Skip those detours.

Life is filled with dreams and possibilities. Spend your dream-time traveling as far as you can; cherish your imagination. Then cherish your reality by taking a small step toward making your dreams come true.

LET GO

It's hard to let go. We often hold on to investments, habits, relationships and defenses long after attaining awareness that they are hurting us.

We notice the problem, like a warning-light going on, then ignore it, hoping by this pretense not to lose all we think is ours.

Investment in the past usually increases our losses, but we still choose the dull ache over the brief confrontation with grief.

It's like keeping yourself on simmer for a lifetime instead of high for a second.

Learn to cut your losses, not hide them. Time to let go and leap forward.

NEPAL JOURNEY II

Flying from Bangkok to Nepal. Waiting with all the other pilgrims for that first view of the Himalayas, "the top of the world." The plane shudders as everyone tries to lean out the windows on the right side.

As the mountains come into view, they seem so much more than mountains to those of us raised with a view of Mount Rainier. Jagged, immense, many Everests, not just one. Mount Everest hardly is noticed amid so many rough giants. I'm out of words, slipping into a trance thinking of all the spires humans create to reach heaven when, as usual, natural architecture is light-years ahead.

The view slips away as we descend through the clouds and drop to views of steeply terraced hillsides, stacked up level upon intricate level until they disappear into the clouds and give way to the Himalayas.

I plan to spend three days seeing Katmandu, Nepal's capital city; then go by bus to the jungle of the Royal Chitwan National Park, near the Nepal-India border; then trek in the Annapurna peaks of the Himalayas.

Katmandu is one grand bazaar of noise and color and smell. Incense, bells, wandering sacred cows, dogs, ducks, chickens and cars all share the streets. Music and garbage everywhere. Spices, textiles, art, all mixed with bicycle parts and American sweatshirts.

I stay at a tiny hotel run by an elegant Hindu woman. The Nepalese I meet are gentle, helpful, and willing to please even though they have seen many Western visitors. One of the streets has been renamed Freak Street in our honor. Most Nepalese speak a little English.

The food is good—rice and oatmeal porridge. Lots of

hot curry and cookies I call "coconut crunchies." I revel in the chance to share other worlds. It amazes me to find the same flowers wherever I travel. The Katmandu market is full of marigolds. Even the smallest hut, no matter how poor, houses a plant or two in a pot on the roof or in front of the door.

UPDATE

When did you last update your perception of your past?

Sometimes we decide the quality of our childhood at 21 and hold onto it as if it were written in stone.

Then we grow, maybe raise our own children, get to know our family in a new way, and re-evaluate.

Negatives become positives. Positives may become negatives. Our perception changes.

Talk to your relatives, gather their views of the past. Try to understand what their motivations and problems were.

A critical mother may have been buckling under her own pain. A tough father may have been terrified for your safety. Love doesn't always end up feeling like love. We all mix up our motivations and make mistakes.

Update, understand, accept, forgive, let go and choose your future.

FILTERS

We've heard that we are what we think, that we get to choose how we see our world.

We know that people often live up or down to our expectations.

Perception is a filter that turns our view toward darkness or light. It can be an open view that sees good things happening, or a closed view that sees only harm and hurt.

So much power.

The power to be open or closed to goodness.

MEDITATION

Meditation is humanity's oldest spiritual discipline. We all know the peace that comes from looking at a still pool, a sunrise, or deep into a flower, or from experiencing the sounds of silence. A moment of pure joy and oneness.

It is the "satori" of Zen, the "samadhi" of the yoga and is a path to St. Paul's "peace that passeth understanding."

Meditation is available in many forms: prayer, star-gazing, deep breathing, chanting, trance or just slowing down.

It reduces tension, enhances awareness of life, increases joy and adds to self-discipline and self-knowledge.

Some call meditation an altered state of consciousness, but it is only the peace waiting beneath the surface of your stress.

A moment of joy, always available as a gift for you, by you, to you and to all of us.

Stop now to sense the rhythm within. Take a deep breath, connect for a moment with all life. The power, the energy, the joy of the whole.

A minute a day for peace.

FAMILY

The next time you find yourself lamenting that your family isn't perfect, remember that you have three families.

First there is the family you are born into, then the surrogate family of friends you may join to survive the transition from your childhood home to your own adult home, and last there is the family you build yourself.

The most important of these families is the one you build yourself. It may include people from the other two, but you get to decide. Think about who you want in your family. What kind of qualities are you looking for? Then gradually add those people to your life. Work on improving relationships with your first two families.

Build a home and family that is safe and loving for you.

Your family is your choice.

VALUES

There is a concern in the land about values. What is happening to people's morals? How can I teach my children values?

There is agreement among some who study human behavior that the development of values can be set up as a sequence of levels, ranked from lowest to highest:

- Fear of punishment.

- Exchange (You give to me, I'll give to you).

- Reciprocity (Meet my expectations, get a reward).

- Law and order (Civilization requires control).

- Principles (I will act according to my beliefs even if I do not personally gain).

- Fairness (the Golden Rule).

- Quality of life for everyone, everywhere.

Check your decisions. On what levels do you make your choices? Very few of us get close even to the level where we act on principles, but we keep trying.

Success is determined by our interaction with living things, not by our collection of inanimate objects. It is the quality of the journey that ultimately brings satisfaction.

PERSPECTIVE

If you wait long enough, things are supposed to look better. It's called perspective, the magic of knowing what matters. The problem is how to get it when you need it.

The next time something happens to get you down, try the "family-album trick."

Imagine yourself 20 years from now sitting in front of the fire reminiscing. Things that were once heartbreakers seem silly or funny. Problems you never thought you could solve worked out. Grief gradually added depth and quality to your life.

Perspective—what made you cry at the age of six is unimportant at 26. Add 20 years to your evaluation of problems and chuckle.

Remind yourself of what is truly important.

Keep the magic in your life.

SELF-ESTEEM

Everything you see, hear, feel and evaluate is filtered through your self-esteem.

Our personal filters are built on a four-fold foundation.

- *Fate:* where you are born, when you are born, whether you are disabled, your race, sex and ethnicity.

- *Family:* rich or poor, supportive or abusive, united or separated.

- *Experience:* how many brick walls you run into, pits you fall into, accidents.

- *Perception:* how you perceive your fate, family and experience.

The most important element in self-esteem is self-perception. The same circumstances produce those who can love and be loved, and those who cannot.

LOVE

Love is all around, yet often we cannot see it.

We imagine love as "the grand passion," the lifetime commitment, not as being available everywhere.

Love is caring and support. It's available from friends, relatives, neighbors, clerks, strangers, colleagues and people who wave from passing tour-buses. You just need to know the rules.

First Rule of Love:
Love is something you do.

All the other rules:
Believe in its presence, make it a priority, assume love will last, share interests, be affectionate, forgive easily, love yourself and share your dreams.

Remember, love is a "game of flex."
Take as many bending-over-backward steps as you can without losing your identity.

FLEXIBILITY

Check your flexibility. Make sure you haven't locked into place.

Every year, do you give every vegetable a second chance? Or did you make your decisions at the age of 12? "Lima beans will never cross my lips."

Do you experiment with new colors? Or do you stick with whatever you decided on at 14? "Plain girls shouldn't wear bright colors."

Do you dream of having everything perfect, clean, orderly? "Why do I have to live with slobs?"

When did you last try a new route to work?

How many friends do you have who are different from you (in race, religion, or ethnicity)?

What new skill did you learn last month?

Check your tension level, shake your shoulders and your mind. Loosen up.

Let the energy of the universe flow through you.

VIEWPOINTS

I just finished a "future" workshop.

I was jogged again into my commitment to try to make a difference. What most of us want, simplified, is peace of mind, peace in the world, and a piece of the action. When we get stuck with a single perspective, the one we were raised with or have held onto from childhood experience, we think it is essential for survival.

All of us need a new viewing point, a way to see alternative strategies.

The lecturer Morris Massey suggests we give ourselves a chance to rise above our limits and history to another point of view, instead of locking into position out of fear and habit.

Relax—use humor, meditate, count to ten, pray, go for a walk or run.

Insulate—find your "hot buttons" and protect them so you can see clearly.

Scan—look at all the possibilities, include every strategy, path, solution, use your imagination.

Empathize—imagine how other people see and feel things, spend a moment on their path with their history.

The truth includes all points of view

GRACE

I want, in fact—to borrow from the language of the saints—to live "in grace" as much of the time as possible. I am not using this term in a strictly theological sense. By grace, I mean an inner harmony, essentially spiritual, which can be translated into outward harmony. I am seeking perhaps what Socrates asked for in the prayer from Phaedrus *when he said, "May the outward and inward man be at one." I would like to achieve a state of inner spiritual grace from which I could function and give as I was meant to in the eye of God.*

Vague as this definition may be, I believe most people are aware of various periods in their lives when they seem to be "in grace" and other periods when they feel "out of grace" even though they may use different words to describe these states. In the first happy condition, one seems to carry all one's tasks before one lightly, as if borne along on a great tide; and in the opposite state one can hardly tie a shoestring.

—ANNE MORROW LINDBERGH,
Gift From the Sea

Whenever I read thoughts on inner peace, I'm struck by the element of choice. We know when we feel centered. We can feel the energy and ecstasy that harmony gives us.

At any given moment, we choose our response. We can choose grace or conflict, positive or negative.

Always reach for the higest-level universe, the one you want to operate in, as much of the time as possible.

HAPPINESS

Happiness is a perception of our minds, not a reflection of our situations. On days when everything goes wrong—days full of mistakes, accidents, rejections, noise—we can still be happy.

Hugh Prather describes a willed mental state, "the grounds for happiness," that passes gently and easily over the endless nonsense that carpets the day.

Be happy being yourself no matter what the day brings.

RISK

Security is mostly a superstition. It does not exist in nature, nor do the children of men as a whole experience it. Avoiding danger is no safer in the long run than outright exposure. Life is either a daring adventure or nothing.
— HELEN KELLER

There is no way to grow and stretch without taking risks. If you want to feel more, be more and give more— it's time to take chances.

The writer David Viscott divides risk into seven phases:

- Recognizing your need to risk
- Deciding to risk
- Initiating the risk
- The point of no return
- Completing the risk
- Adapting to the change
- Evaluating the results

Start now with the baby steps. As you become more comfortable trusting yourself, you can take bigger ones.

Give yourself a chance.

CHOICE

We are all able to choose happiness, but most of us prefer not to. We are stuck in patterns of guilt and recrimination.

There are many examples of people who have chosen peace and joy in the midst of loss. It doesn't lessen the loss, it just gives what remains value.

Here are some I know of either personally or by their public image:

Martin Luther King, Sr.	Gloria Vanderbilt
Helen Keller	Mother Teresa
Ted Kennedy, Jr.	Jacques Cousteau
Harriet Tubman	Sam Smith
Py Bateman	Betty Ford
Maya Angelou	Max Clelland
Patricia Neal	Terry Fox
Dan Deardorff	Anne Jillian
Anne Morrow Lindbergh	John Merrick (The Elephant Man)
William Least Heat Moon	Jill Kinmont

Make up your own list of people you know. Then add your self to it.

SEPTEMBER

September is one of my favorite times because it promises a new beginning just when I begin to think how I will miss summer. While others go off to school, start on a journey of your own, a journey toward self-knowledge and intimacy.

The more I am truly myself, the more I can truly be one with you. The more I am truly one with you, the more I can be truly myself . . . High monogamy . . . requires that we look directly and unflinchingly at our every weakness . . . to the very heart of our intentionality.
—GEORGE LEONARD

What do you know about your intentionality? Leonard says the examination takes vertiginous daring. Vertiginous translates as "whirling or dizzying," and sounds wonderful. Join me in a personal class, a vertiginous examination of our intentionality, or simply the journey toward the heart.

WINNING

"We were a little tentative in the first half," Seahawks quarterback Dave Krieg said. "I was throwing off my back foot. Sometimes when you want to do everything just right, you play it too close to the vest."

The game improved after coach Chuck Knox delivered a halftime message, Krieg said, "to go out and have fun, to let it go."

Watch out for the serious this season. Remember to relax, chuckle, sing, appreciate the light side. Let it go, let it happen, let it in. That's how most of us win, and even if we don't, we know we won't lose.

CRITICISM

According to parenting and management theories, criticism has lost power recently as a way to control others. Encouragement works much better. But it's hard to change the patterns of a lifetime.

Much of our history has been spent struggling. We weren't thinking about the quality of life, only of survival. Criticism was used to control and motivate children. We wanted them to be tough enough for a difficult world.

Our survival needs have changed. We've begun to evaluate quality, to talk about love, personal awareness, relationships, communication and family strength. Instead of a negative power over others, we talk of empowering others.

Criticism is dysfunctional. It builds resentment and fear, and undermines confidence. We now have a world where inner strength is essential to success.

Love, support, and encouragement help build values important to the quality of our future, values that will reduce personal violence, not increase it.

Let go of the negative. Survival now is much more likely to depend on the positive.

NEPAL JOURNEY III

Katmandu is still ringing in my ears, but it's time to board a bus to southern Nepal and the National Wildlife Refuge. Nepalese roads are amazingly steep. Just imagine a multiplication of the old Lewiston grade in Idaho, add incredible steep cliffs and no shoulders and then close your eyes.

There are very few roads in southern Nepal, and none in the north, because of the mountains. Many people still walk everywhere and I pass many travellers trudging up and down the hills.

People who ride do so in gaudily decorated 1940s-vintage square trucks. Big trucks, like army transport vehicles, with people and goods stuffed in the back.

The farms we pass are the same terraces I glimpsed from the plane. Very much like China, a patch-work quilt but with many more levels. Lots of water buffalos, and no evidence of mechanization except the occasional car on the road.

Many parts of Nepal are referred to by the euphemism "food-deficit area"—to indicate that people are barely surviving. But southern Nepal looks more productive and less close to the poverty line. Produce is everywhere; melons grow even on people's roofs.

Nepal is one of the most beautiful places I have ever been. Poinsettas seem as big as houses and orchids hang out of the trees. At the road-end I am picked up by a land rover to ford the river and cross into the park and jungle.

My home is now a small cabin along side a broad river, and in the dusk I can see the jungle across the river and hear the elephants trumpeting.

My internal clock is dizzy, so I awaken just before dawn and creep out to sit by the Dungre River, which flows by the camp. Fog is slowly rising, herons are fishing and a crew of elephants is already at work with the *manhout* in charge, gathering food for the elephant camp. The elephants carry huge tree-branches to forage on.

At breakfast I meet Maria, after I am attracted to her small table by the energy she throws around the room. She is 71, a Hungarian gymnastics teacher who has just climbed all the way to the Everest base-camp near the border with China. Full of the adventure, she describes the beauty of the mountains and tells of the trekker who died on the trail she was on. Two or three of every thousand trekkers die because of the altitude and lack of transportation or medical care, she notes. "Not to worry," she then says to me.

I'm a little uncomfortable at a jungle camp designated for tourists, but the guides are naturalists or seem to be well-informed, and the money paid for camping privileges is used to preserve the refuge.

The day includes a ride in the jungle behind the ears of an elephant. It's like bareback riding, except on a bigger back. The fog is still with us as my elephant crunches into the jungle. I'm thinking "lions and tigers and bears," but in fact we see deer, rhinoceroses and peacocks.

Another dawn; steam is rising from the jungle as penny-sized drops of dew plummet down on me from the trees. I'm thinking about the New Year. Last night was spent talking with Australians, Nepalese and Indians, and in thinking: "What are you going to give to the world next year? How will you keep your give-and-take in balance?"

I am beginning to slip into Nepalese time, to relax. There is no sense of impending Armageddon here. Time will continue to unfold and re-cycle.

It is time to leave the jungle and head to the mountains. I cannot wait to launch myself into the sky like a paper airplane. The bus leaves me in Pokhara, a jump-off city for trekkers. Looming high above the town is the first Himalayan peak I see from land, Machhapuchare, "The Fishtail," 22,940 feet high. It is breathtaking, pink and utterly magnificent at dusk.

Trudging to my lodging through the dusty, dirty, anything but picturesque town, I am startled when I find I must cross a small lake on a tiny raft to reach my hotel, the Fishtail Lodge.

FORGIVE

You did the best you could with who you were and what you knew at the time. As soon as you learned something better, you did that.

So why can't you forgive yourself and others for past mistakes?

For some people, punishment is not enough, atonement insufficient, retribution never satisfying. They wallow in guilt. They refuse to forgive themselves or others. They lose the future because they are trapped in the past.

Search out the painful mistakes in your past and prepare a certificate of forgiveness, complete with a gold seal for each one.

Maybe you'll give one to an adult child:

"I did the best I could. I wasn't a perfect parent. Here's a blanket apology . . . Let's end the criticism."

Give one to your spouse to end some past recrimination.

Give one to yourself: "I'm not perfect. I made a mistake."

Create your certificates, forgive yourself. Then, sit down, relax, breathe deeply.

Let go of the guilt, let go of the past, breathe in the present and stay open to your future.

WOODENHEADEDNESS

Folly, as defined by historian Barbara Tuchman, is the pursuit of a policy contrary to your self-interest. Folly occurs when we seek power, ignore evidence, lack flexibility and are unable to reverse. She calls it "woodenheadedness."

It's a lot easier to get your way if you have more than one way!

A VISION STATEMENT

Spring is a powerful motivator. So much energy is loose, and there is anticipation of more to come. It is a time of visions.

Across America, corporations are examining their businesses and formulating vision statements. They want to join all their employees together with a clear direction. It keeps the momentum rolling.

Nations and religions do it, too, with drama and music. Singing "America the Beautiful" or "The Battle Hymn of the Republic" reminds us of our cultural vision. It unites and motivates.

It's harder to put together a personal vision statement, to chart your course in a clear way. Can you describe your vision, not as a goal, but as a way of life?

Reach deep within to find a clear statement of your values. Work on it until it wakes you up in the morning and helps you sleep at night. Fine-tune your vision until you find peace and passion living by it. Write down a statement, a short one, that meets the following criteria for you:

- Provides a definition of success
- Gives you a sense of quality
- Makes decisions easier
- Gives you a sense of fulfillment now
- Creates future vision
- Gives you a feeling of charity

- Allows you to handle ambivalence
- Gives you power
- Generates personal energy
- Connects deeply within

There is no deadline here. It is a lifetime assignment.

ZOOS

What's your view of zoos? Some resent the cages, however contrived they are to seem natural. A polar bear should sit on ice, not concrete. A gorilla deserves more than just a few friends. And what if the giraffe doesn't like her mate?

Others have slowly come to believe, with some grief, that zoos—preferably good zoos—are becoming, along with parks and refuges, the repository for the wild animals of the world. Animals we cannot eat, wear, pet, or work will eventually run out of space. There is not room for all of us, and our first commitment is to humans.

Yet adult humans appear to have a choice of circumstance and zoo animals do not. They depend on our willingness to care for them.

The quality of our zoos is a test of our grace.

BALANCE

Everything seems to speed up in the fall. Cool weather changes our metabolism. Summer, winding down, changes our perceptions. The temptation is to speed toward Christmas, then collapse and start over with the New Year.

It's time for a stress inoculation.

Assume you'll be out of breath and plan for it. Take out your calendar and set aside mini-vacations, afternoons of solitude, hours of silence, novels to read, massages, gentle walks, cups of herb tea, moments to choose peace.

Pleasure and productivity depend on a balance within you, set by you, for you.

GOOD AND EVIL

If only there were evil people somewhere insidiously committing evil deeds and it were necessary only to separate them from the rest of us and destroy them. But the line dividing good and evil cuts through the heart of every human being. And who is willing to destroy a piece of his own heart?

—ALEXANDER SOLZHENITSYN, *The Gulag Archipelago*

NEW AGE

There is so much misinterpretation of "New Age" philosophy that I want to write about it. Many people refuse to blend the best of their past views with the best of any new view. They think one has to accept a new perspective as gospel, and forsake all others. "New Age" ideas are just another set of tools for coping with the universe: new tools to put with the ones you already have.

First you have to meet the basic demands of life—for food, shelter and personal security—then you can check out your perspective and evaluate whether it emphasizes joy or sorrow.

It is possible to work on the real pain and problems of life while believing in and trying to live the ideal of the love among us. It is not an either-or situation. I think we resist the very simplicity of the choices we have. We prefer the answers to be deeper, harder, more complex. We prefer joy wrought from pain, like blood out of a stone, to joy accepted as the air we breathe.

We hold on to our suffering. It is familiar, an old predictable friend. It hurts less than the pain of change.

I do not suggest you leave your forts and your usual coping tools, only that you open the windows and look at new possibilities.

Most of the wonderful steps we've taken toward a better understanding of life were once someone's crackpot dreams.

CRAP

No one can make you feel inferior without your consent.
—ELEANOR ROOSEVELT

It's not easy to decide on your value and hold on to it. Have you ever been sailing through a day, when suddenly a sharp word brought you down?

We give other people tremendous power over our perspective. Even when we are at our peaks, feeling clear, we allow their views to cloud our own.

Put together a perspective survival kit. You can memorize it or carry it with you—a phrase, a poem, a place, a taste, a sound, a picture, a smell, a person, a skip, a hug, a shrug, a letter, a deep breath, a warmth from another time.

If all that is too touch-feelie for you, just remember—when people put crap in your cup, don't drink it!

EGO OR SPIRIT

The choice is always there: to build or tear down.

The ego tries to make all that surrounds us fit our comfort zone and beliefs about our value. The spirit desires to create security by giving ourselves and others acceptance.

Ego wants to blame, to stake out turf and defend it. Spirit wants to accept, forgive and work for a better future.

Your moment-to-moment contacts with life give you the opportunity to choose ego or spirit, love or fear.

A quick intake of breath, as you decide what you will be and what we are.

"Let us build the earth by building one another."
—Pierre Teilhard De Chardin

HOLIDAYS

Holiday time is here: so is the challenge to treat one another with grace, and to remember the importance of the connections between us.

It isn't easy, so here are a few rules for relatives:

- Take very good care of yourself so you aren't stressed-out and crabby.

- Don't expect or attempt perfection; settle for anything short of a disaster.

- Don't ask if the pies are homemade.

- Don't correct or criticize anyone.

- Choose to be happy, not right.

- Don't care who gets the credit for whatever.

- Avoid competition and comparison; don't keep score.

- Give up playing martyr or victim.

- When in doubt, keep quiet.

- Remember, very few things are truly important.

Then thank everyone for staying alive so you can love or hate them for another year. Your relatives may not be perfect, but they are yours.

CHRISTMAS

Christmas can seem overwhelming if you miss the gift it promises. The holidays offer a rebirth of spirit at the coldest season of the year, the winter before the spring.

You are asked to see and hear the beauty all around, the love within. Christmas is a time to move closer to one another, generate warmth, celebrate life.

There is only one thing that can stop the Christmas spirit: the speed at which you travel through the season.

The music is there if you take the time to listen. The spirit is there if you take the time to let it touch your heart. The beauty is there if you give yourself time to see.

The commercialization of Christmas is an injection of speed that you can bypass. Walk slower, feel more, do less. You can have the spirit for nothing more than your time.

Give yourself time for Christmas.

COURAGE

There are many kinds of courage we share. The "flash" courage that saves a life. The big courage of revolution. The everyday courage it takes to get out of bed and read the newspaper. As Amy Cross, a writer, puts it, "The courage to be ordinary and to be strange. To think one's own thoughts. To endure uncertainty."

Courage is the opposite of the instinct to keep everything under control. It is against inertia and death. It is toward intensity and life.

Courage takes center stage, if only for brief moments. It cannot survive sidelines, corners, waiting to be saved. It is upright, unbroken. The little courages of your life add up to big courage over time.

Resist the offers of small, safe quarters in your mind.

THE ROLE OF VICTIM

When we are young and someone attacks us, we don't ask many questions. We are surprised.

When we grow up the questions start. We are able to separate ourselves from our circumstances. We learn that we are old enough to protect ourselves. We can no longer pretend to be unaware of reality. We give up the illusions.

Letting go of the role of victim, growing up, means no longer acting surprised.

LIGHT

Summer brings so much light there is a chance to clean out our minds. Illumination prompts us to clean the rooms, the dusty corners of our perceptions.

Clean the windows. Better yet, open them. Throw out the rubbish, bury it in the garden, all the old painful memories, miscellaneous guilts, and little resentments.

Interview your soul. Let in the light. You can see for miles.

IMAGINARY JUNGLES

I was once asked to speak at a meeting of very successful men and their wives. They were all corporate presidents in the highest financial brackets. The topic they wanted me to discuss was "Self-Esteem in the Jungle." As I walked into this posh hotel, past Mercedes, BMWs, and two Rolls Royces, I wondered at the topic.

In the elegant conference room I questioned them. What do you mean by "jungle"? They answered, "The corporate jungle." Were there dangers lurking in the hallway, the boardroom, the elevators? When I imagine a jungle I think of danger, wild animals, lack of shelter, and not knowing where your next meal is coming from. I don't imagine corporate boardrooms. When you are more than a generation past poverty, you may need to create a feeling that you are still in a battle for your life; otherwise the constant pursuit of money seems meaningless.

Sometimes when we are removed from basic survival issues we create false ones. We feel threatened, we think we are in danger when we are not. We don't pursue other values.

It's time to stop and find out where the real dangers are. When we lose track of our life-force we lose track of ourselves.

HAVENS

One of the most important things we do is create our homes. They are not places for others to see, but our havens, places of safety and life. Look around and check whether there is a match between you and your environment.

Each of us has his own patterns in his mind and heart. My home is filled with birds, plants, animals, water, color, scents, prisms, crystals, mobiles, fish, colored glass, snow-filled globes, books, and spiders weaving their webs. I love everything living—even mold. My home does not look like a picture in a magazine.

Build, design, paint, sew, and dig around your place until it is truly yours. If you share rooms, create a corner just for you.

You can never return to the comfort of the womb, or even of childhood, but you can get close.

NEPAL JOURNEY IV

I start this day with porridge and watch my first sunrise over the Himalayas. Oatmeal always reminds me of my mother and cold mornings in Spokane. I am a little apprehensive after meeting with Minma, the Sherpa guide with whom I will travel.

He speaks little English, and wants to take a trail I fear is too difficult for me. We compromise, and the porridge bolsters my faith in this trip. It's like carrying mother in my stomach. She helped instill in me this sense of adventure, so I'm glad she's in my thoughts.

Minma and I set off together. My backpack of about 30 pounds holds my water, clothing, flashlight, knife, instant coffee and cup, first-aid kit, a few small oranges and my new down vest. Minma's pack holds food, a small tent, sleeping bags and extra boots.

We walk through the bazaar, the Tibetan refugee camp, across a valley and to the end of the road, where there are other trekking groups of about 25 people, including porters and guides. I prefer just me.

This is the point of commitment. There will be no more vehicles of any kind; the paths are narrow and steep. A group of small pack-horses passes by with bells ringing carrying A.I.D. (Agency for International Development) rice from Japan.

I climb until I am counting steps, resting and counting another fifty. In four hours I climb 3,000 feet.

Multiple terraces as far as I can see. The path is so steep that it is made of rock steps with grooves worn by centuries of hooves and bare feet. This is the main trade route through Nepal between India and Tibet, and merchants and travelers have walked this path for three thousand years.

At the top of this pass we camp on a ledge that seems to overlook all of Nepal. The clouds part, and I can reach out and almost touch the jagged peaks.

There's no way I can describe these mountains. They make beautiful Mountain Rainier look like a seed pearl next to these immense, roughly cut diamonds.

At the ocean, the other extreme, I always feel like a grain of sand caught in a brief moment of endless time. The feeling is stronger here. These mountains have been here forever and are untouched, unworn, as if they had risen out of the earth in a jagged thrust only moments ago. The Himalayas were formed when the subcontinents of India and China crashed together. So much power in a landscape of such peace.

It will take 25 days to reach the Tibetan border by foot, depending on weather and speed. Two months would take me through Tibet and into China. I am only going halfway, but already I want to come back and go further.

Time to crawl into my sleeping bag, mind boggled, muscles complaining of disuse followed by misuse. Time to sleep under the stars, so big and so close they seem only a cold puff of breath away.

GROWING OLD

We're all getting older. There are rewards and trade-offs, but there is also loss. Pretending it's not there can leave us unable to make the transition, and unexpectedly depressed. This is a culture that rewards youth and beauty, and it is unlikely to change anytime soon.

Having laid out that truth, I can counter it with the incredible pleasures that come with the deepening of self that is part of long life-experience: self-knowledge, stronger values, a sense of personal honor, awareness of competence, independence, freedom from competition, and an identity separate from the opposite sex—all are wonders of getting older.

Research on "happiness scales" indicates that if your health remains good, your happiest years are the sixties and seventies. There are many reasons cited, but the one that stands out is that there is no one left to push you around. Some of us reach sixty before we feel we truly run our own lives.

The key is just that: running your own life. If you continue to live by others' expectations or your culture's definition of your worth, ageing will be hell. Put some energy into deciding what you want to do.

Create an image of yourself ten years into the future. Make it a decade filled with possibilities instead of losses.

THAT WORD

Love. Poor word, so often dismissed with a snort. Love—What that hell can that do? Well, if you feel it, you find it becomes everything. It's included in the answer to every question and hidden in the secrets of every confusing problem. And if you don't feel it, it's something somebody else is talking about: "There they go again, talking about love."

—AUTHOR/LECTURER TOM RUSK

"ENEMIES"

I sometimes advocate the development of people who don't like you. They can be a great source of energy and a testing of your quality as a person. Think of all the energy you can derive from an "enemy." "She's so bad, and I'm so good." You can almost feel the rush of self-righteousness. Always choose good, strong people to dislike. Don't bother with clearly unethical people. You don't want to exchange energy with people you cannot admire on at least some level.

Don't keep the same ones around too long, because they lose their juice. Try and recycle them every year so you can learn new things about yourself.

Don't keep too many going at one time, It's a sign that you are more than just independent and opinionated. Try to limit your list of known enemies to five. (You cannot bother with the unknown.) When it gets up to six, take one out to lunch. You two have a lot in common or you wouldn't have such strong feelings.

CHEAP THRILLS

One summer, when I was a little girl, my family spent two weeks at a cabin on Newman Lake, outside of Spokane. I would float on my back in the water, feeling free and weightless. Iridescent blue dragonflies would land on me and I was amazed. Their color was so intense it was magic.

Another summer, many years and miles from that lake, the magic returned. I was lying next to a small pond we had dug in our backyard when a dragonfly landed. I wanted to believe it had flown all the way from Newman Lake.

It delivered a powerful thrill as it touched my arm. The feeling ran through my body—like a sexual experience. I ran into the house and told my husband what had happened. He looked at me, smiled, and said, "Jennifer, you are so easy to please!"

I hesitated, then agreed. You bet I am! If you're not easy to thrill, it doesn't happen often.

TRAVEL

If you don't travel you miss the history within your bones. You settle for a backyard instead of the world.

Travel reminds you of beauty, possibility, all the rhythms of the spirit. Other ways, languages, temperatures and foods let you find new ways within yourself. The people you glimpse, meet or touch become part of what you are— richer, deeper.

The things that keep you home—fear, inflexibility, bias, the unknown—keep you away from your true home. The world is where the heart is.

FEEL THE BALANCE

The days whiz by, out of control. When are you going to slow down and feel balance within your heart?

- As soon as I finish this list.
- When the house is done.
- It will be easier when the kids are older.
- I need more money to feel safe.
- When I retire.

How about right now? A friend of mine who is 80 reminded me recently that we always think we're short of money, but we're much more likely to be short of time.

SAFETY STRATEGIES

Most of what we do is designed to keep us safe. We want to feel, deep inside, that we cannot be hurt again.

Some of us find safety in control over inanimate objects, some with money, others by holding tight to a relationship.

Your safety strategy is usually a response to whatever made you feel unsafe as a child. It is an old survival strategy.

What helps you to feel safe inside? Why? What is the personal history behind your strategy? Is it working for you now?

Remind yourself over and over: I am grown, I can take care of myself, I am safe.

CHILDHOOD DUES

The truth about our childhood is stored up in our body, and although we can repress it, we can never alter it. Our intellect can be deceived, our feelings manipulated, our perceptions confused, and our body tricked with medication. But someday the body will present its bill, for it is as incorruptible as a child who, still whole in spirit, will accept no compromises or excuses, and it will not stop tormenting us until we stop evading the truth.

—ALICE MILLER

GRADUATION PATCHES

I once asked a therapist why he couldn't issue graduation cards, as Red Cross life-saving courses do, so you knew when you were done. I wanted a little card I could carry in my wallet to show people I was complete.

I then suggested that I would do without the card if he would guarantee to make me as good as new. He said that wasn't possible either. The most he could offer was to patch the broken places. Then I would be strong, like the knees of jeans.

We are all bumped and bruised. The patches mark the depth of our experience. None of us gets a card for living unless we issue it to ourselves.

BUILDING LOVE

It's such a hunger—wanting to be loved. When it doesn't come early—from parents or peers—we think it never will. There is a hollowness, an emptiness that penetrates unexpectedly and leaves us catching our breath.

The hollowness inside is made by the illusion of unconditional love and the inability to accept the love that's available. The attempt to replace the irreplaceable.

Remember, when you are hurting, the stages of grief: denial, anger, bargaining, acceptance and re-building. Grieve for what never was. Build love into your life now. It's all that's available. It's enough.

NEPAL JOURNEY V

The days become an enchanting series of highs and lows. Up thousands of steps and then descending the same number into small villages. The village of Birathanti is especially beautiful. It lies beyond a cable bridge, suspended over a raging river, and looks like a paradise painted by Gauguin: bright flowers and fabrics, doorways and windows painted in bright designs—all edged by waterfalls. Hot tea, Tibetan fry bread, and the chance to rest.

After several days my senses catch up with me and I force myself to bathe in one of the icy streams that carry water from the Annapurna snows. Yikes!

Tonight the stars are even more incredible, the sky so clear and deep. Orion looks as it must have to herdsman long ago. Close enough to feel the warrior's breath and count the jewels in his scabbard. Cephia, the queen, looks real as she lounges only inches above the mountain peaks.

I'm sleeping in a farmyard near the water buffalos. I've filled my water bottle with hot water and rolled it to the bottom of my sleeping bag. Ecstasy.

The trail is so beautiful, valley upon valley, waterfalls more beautiful than any I have ever seen, as I climb hour upon hour straight up. It must be obvious to everyone that you would have to go up and down on this path, but it just dawns on me today. The first great breakthough— "The Himalayas are up and down." It seems profound only if your body is involved. Nothing I read had prepared me for the steepness.

The subject of suffering comes to mind. There are, of course, two kinds of suffering, that which has a reward and that which doesn't. I've always tried to avoid the latter—

time to pull out the chocolate bar I stashed in my pack back in Seattle.

Minma was prepared to cook all the meals, but after several days we began eating most meals in what are called "tea" houses, thatched homes in small towns along the trail which cater to trekkers.

The food is heavy with grains (oatmeal and breads of all sorts), vegetables (often covered with a mildly spiced curry sauce), lots of eggs and an occasional chicken. Some small apples and oranges are available, but never milk.

I compare notes and eat with trekkers from all over the world at these tea houses. But as we climb higher and farther, we meet fewer and fewer people on the trail.

Minma, about 30 and a farmer when he's not a guide, is like a shadow to me. He speaks a little English, but we never really chat.

At rest, after nine hours of climbing, I sit with the stars again.

Sleep is easy to come by here. It is so quiet that a hen and her seven chicks settle in only an arm's length away. Lentils and rice settle easily in my full stomach.

THE MYSTICAL EXPERIENCE

The most beautiful and most profound emotion we can experience is the sensation of the mystical. It is the sower of the true science. He to whom this emotion is a stranger—who can no longer stand wrapped in awe—is as good as dead. That deeply emotional conviction of the presence of a superior reasoning power which is revealed in the incomprehensible universe forms my idea of God.

—ALBERT EINSTEIN

THE MOMENT

An important life-skill, and the skill of a philosopher, is the ability to separate one's self from the moment.

We are all tempted to feel desperate about our*selves* when what we actually face is the pain of the single moment we're in.

When depression, stress, or grief hits, don't think it's the way life is. It's not. The moment will pass.

INTELLECTUAL CHASTITY

Scepticism is the chastity of the intellect, and it is shameful to surrender it too soon or to the first comer: there is nobility in preserving it coolly and proudly through long youth, until at last, in the ripeness of instinct and discretion, it can be safely exchanged for fidelity and happiness.

—GEORGE SANTAYANA,
Scepticism and Animal Faith

HEROIC ACTS

What we each choose to do with our psychological life is of historic import. When you break or transform a negative family pattern, you change history. When you realize a source of pain and limitation, you turn on a light for all who follow.

Take the time, and care, to understand your family patterns, or you will repeat them and be unaware that you are your father (or mother), setting up similar injustices and barriers.

Accept the power you have to contribute to our world. Your willingness to change is not merely a personal analytical problem, it is a heroic step toward freeing others from the pattern of many generations before you.

RHYTHMS

Drip, drip, gentle mist — a different rhythm. It seems I'm happiest when my life matches the timing of the rain.

I love grey days. I think it's a matter of pace. When we find and live the rhythm within, we are at peace.

Do you know your pace? At what speed are you in tune? It's not easy to remember. Yet, it's a crucial element of being your own person.

Slow your life down or speed it up to resonate with the best of your own heart.

TRANSITION

I've written about letting go of the weight of the past—
how about the weight of the day?

We're usually tired or a little stressed at the end of the
day, and are tempted to carry that weight into the night.

You can change that with relinquishment. Wonderful
word, relinquishment. Sounds like what it means. Here are
some ideas:

- Load all the tensions of the day into an imaginary
  rocket and blast it off to the moon.

- On a cold day write "blech!" on a piece of paper
  and send it up the chimney.

- Blow it all into a balloon and let it go.

- Put it down the garbage disposal.

- Wash it off in the shower.

- Sweat it away with exercise.

- Put it into a boat of leaves and sail it out to sea.

- Grind it up or sand it down to nothing.

- Dig a hole and bury it.

Don't try to drink it, eat it, or fuss it away. Lift everything from your mind and shoulders at least once a day just
so you can remember how good it feels and that you know
how to do it.

There must be fifty ways to leave your bother.

SHARING AND SOLITUDE

There are many reasons it is hard to stand alone. One is the need for witnesses to our own life. A strong feeling hits us, and we turn for someone to share it with or validate it. A beautiful scene lies before us, and it seems to offer less if other eyes don't see it, too.

Why can't we feel and see with the same intensity alone? Are we the victims of too much romance and not enough joy? Sunsets that are for two, not one? How many moments of passion slip by because the right number are not present?

It is possible to both share and not share. It is possible to enjoy the music with companions and to go deeper, to hear the oboe, alone.

You can do and be both. It is not lonely to be alone. There is only one person who will fully know or care about the intensity of your life experience. Share when you can. Share what you can. But remember solitude. Remember, always, you are the only witness.

A MATTER OF PERSPECTIVE

Years ago I used to notice the differences among motormen on the Indiana Avenue streetcar line in Chicago — a street often blocked by badly parked cars and huge trailer trucks backing into warehouses and maneuvering in everybody's way. Some motormen seemed to expect to be able to drive down Indiana Avenue without interruption. Every time they got blocked, they would get steamed up with rage, clang their bells and lean out of their cars to shout at the truck drivers. At the end of a day these motormen must have been nervous wrecks; I can imagine them coming home at the end of the day, jittery and hypertensive, a menace to their wives and children. Other motormen, however, seemed to expect Indiana Avenue to be heavily blocked — a realistic expectation, because it usually was. They could sit and wait for minutes without impatience, calmly whistling a tune, cleaning their fingernails, or writing their reports. In other words, confronting the same objective situation, some motormen lived a hellish life of anger and nervous tension, other motormen had a nice, relaxing job, with plenty of time to rest.

—S. I. Hayakawa,
Symbol, Status, and Personality

LUCKY

Every so often I get a letter that points out that I've been lucky. "Things have worked out for you."

There are those who think it's easy to look on the bright side when everything goes well in your life. They say the true test is when adversity strikes. Do you have the courage to be happy then?

The issue is not perspective but fate, they say. Instead of talking philosophy, just show gratitude when things go your way.

It has never occurred to me to write for those who had it all, knew it, and were happy about it, too.

I think and write for people like me, facing the mundane ups and downs of the average life. We don't have the monumental agony and ecstasy of Michaelangelo, just a little of both.

I concentrate on making the most of our joy in what we have, what's within, what surrounds us, what we can imagine, what we can help make happen. I try to show how to survive with peace and pleasure intact until the last breath.

Maybe we cannot control fate, but we can control how we see it and what we do with it.

THE OTHER INSURANCE

We're surrounded everywhere by advice on how to save money, invest money, and "roll over" money for better interest rates. Some of you consider yourself thoughtful, informed money managers, and spend time every day or every week reviewing your portfolio.

Many people buy insurance to cover every possibility. They are protected against fire, flood, accident, the deaths of others, disability, even "acts of God."

All this care and protection to maintain our financial security is important, but there may be a flaw in your planning.

The insurance problem is not always fate; it is in the unpredictability of relationships. Divorce or estrangement costs far more than a bad investment.

Take the same care, time and energy every day of every week to review your relationship portfolio. Put together a little inner insurance to protect yourself against the high cost of personal mistakes.

VISITATION

There is much talk these days of "channeling," of contact with spirits. Some people are sure they can feel the wisdom of other generations. Others believe none of it.

Most of us, though, can accept, by whatever medium, the importance of learning from the past: other worlds, other observers, other spirits who have faced difficult times and survived.

I share with you here a poem on one of the spirits among us. We learn so slowly.

Abraham Lincoln Walks At Midnight
(In Springfield, Illinois)

It is portentous, and a thing of state
That here at midnight, in our little town
A mourning figure walks, and will not rest,
Near the old court-house pacing up and down,

Or by his homestead, or in shadowed yards
He lingers where his children used to play,
Or through the market, on the well-worn stones
He stalks until the dawn-stars burn away.

A bronzed, lank man! His suit of ancient black,
A famous high top-hat and plain worn shawl
Make him the quaint great figure that men love,
The prairie-lawyer, master of us all.

He cannot sleep upon his hillside now,
He is among us:—as in times before!
And we who toss and lie awake for long
Breathe deep, and start, to see him pass the door.

His head is bowed. He thinks on men and kings.
Yea, when the sick world cries, how can he sleep?
Too many peasants fight, they know not why,
Too many homesteads in black terror weep.

The sins of all the war-lords burn his heart.
He sees the dreadnoughts scouring every main.
He carries on his shawl-wrapped shoulders now
The bitterness, the folly and the pain.

He cannot rest until a spirit-dawn
Shall come;—the shining hope of Europe free:
The league of sober folk, the Workers' Earth,
Bringing long peace to Cornland, Alp and Sea.

It breaks his heart that kings must murder still,
That all his hours of travail here for men
Seem yet in vain. And who will bring white peace
That he may sleep upon his hill again?

—Vachel Lindsay,
1914

RESILIENCE

This is a day to check your resilience. How easily do you bounce back when you are a witness to what is, not what could be?

Resilience is a choice. Avoid the temptation to lock in and burn out. Don't choose fatigue and frustration because your actions don't bring the expected reward.

Some of us forget who's in control. We literally don't know what it is to feel normal and healthy. You may think burn-out is life. You end up in a holding pattern.

We flinch at the daily news because we cannot discern the meaning of our actions in the world where the significance of a single life is still unclear.

Take action, return to your center, and hold on to your balance. We all travel back and forth between the reality we can control and the reality beyond our power.

Return to familiar rituals that bring a measure of peace. Take care of your mind and body. Create order and grace in your world. Hold on to your passion and the fleeting moments of joy.

Resilience depends on your ability to give yourself life. Your ability to care for others is wholly dependent on it.

INTIMACY IS LIFE

Itimacy—knowing, being known, time, trust, commitment and love.

Most of us want to pass through life known by at least one other person. We want, maybe even yearn for, the magic of intimacy—yet we keep people at bay. It's a tremendous loss because in doing so we also keep ourselves at bay. What you are willing to risk in your relationships with others is a measure of how deeply you are willing to know yourself.

We keep ourselves and others away by skating on the surface. There is never enough time or energy for intimacy. It is a low priority because we are preoccupied. We become spectators—watching our interactions with others, manipulating, measuring the external. Perfectionism, criticism, competition and impatience set up life as a bus, traveling at top speed, going through the motions, to where?

We consider affairs because of the thrill of not being known, of being "close" to a stranger. You can move on before he sees you or you see him clearly. We keep busy for the same reason.

Intimacy takes time and risk. You need to give loyalty, acceptance, tolerance and yourself. Be transparent, despite the vulnerability. Intimacy is the measure of the depth and quality you will allow in your life, within yourself and with others. It grows over a lifetime.

It is life, the knowing and loving of what you are.

NEPAL JOURNEY VI

Today another hard climb: 6,000 feet. We reach the village where we will camp, and I climb another 1,000 feet to the top of Pun Hill, which is 10,200 feet high with a 360 degree view of the mountains. Peak after peak surrounding me. The guide tells me that every year the King of Nepal comes here by helicopter to survey his land. It is freezing on this hilltop and there is ice on the puddles when I climb down and into my sleeping bag. Many nights we sleep under the stars. When it's cold or rainy, we use the tent or sleep in closet-size rooms in people's houses open to trekkers.

The Nepalese have a better way of keeping warm. They are dancing in the hut next door. Stamping their feet, beating drums, chanting, laughing, late into the night. I fall asleep to their drums.

The trail today winds down into a valley that reminds me of the rain forests of the Olympic Peninsula. It feels like a jungle, moss hanging from trees, ferns everywhere. I keep passing water buffalos. They use neither harness nor nose ring here. Their buffalos look fierce, but are very gentle. All of the many animals I have encountered on this trek are gentle. Gentle people, gentle animals. I have yet to see or hear a squabble, a raised voice, a whip or stick being used. The animals are everywhere, as we pass through villages, on the path, in the house, all with young nearby. Chickens, ducks, pigs, dogs, small horses, burros and water buffalos. Along all the paths I travel I am greeted, even by small children, with hands together as in prayer, head gently bowed, and the word "namaste." The greeting translates as "I salute the Spirit within you."

The forest I am walking through today is full of rhododendrons, orange trees and orchids, an unexpected combination.

My feet are beginning to drag when another trekker passing tells me there is a hot spring outside of the next town, Tatopani. Just one hill and a cable bridge away. The dust of a week disappears in a Nepalese hot tub.

I feel at home now. My muscles are shaping up, I can walk ten miles a day even if it is up and down. I like the food, the hot dal sauce (lentil-based) over rice, fried potatoes and oranges. Not much variety, but fine with me. Some moleskin on a blister is the only reminder that this is new work for me.

Tonight I sleep near a buffalo again. He snores. I wonder if I do at high altitudes. I don't dream at night here—or I'm not remembering dreams like I do at home. I'm finally living one of my dreams. The tension has melted away.

The message that comes to me here is one we all know well: Body, mind, earth—keep the connections strong . . .

Dawn. I am moving by 5 AM. Holding a cup of tea to keep warm. It is freezing at night, but warms to a sunny 60 to 70 degrees most days. I find myself stripping down to shorts and a shirt by midday, but adding a jacket and long pants when the sun drops behind a mountain for the night.

We're moving up and out of the valley now, climbing higher and higher, but the elevation changes are more gradual. We will soon be above the tree line as the forest shifts to evergreens and scrub.

There are very few trekkers on the trail now. It is late in the year, and we are eight days from a transportation point. We pass small groups of Tibetan nomads on horseback, laughing and teasing each other. Herds of small shaggy goats carrying packs trot by, followed by their kids. I sit on the ground and one tiny one comes up and nuzzles me. I cuddle him, but realize I could never get *this* kid past customs.

The mountains around me seem closer each day; they are so high, the gorges so deep, the cliffs so jagged—everything is exaggerated. There are a thousand Yosemite Falls tumbling down these cliffs. I am surrounded by snow and water. Rivers no one could raft, fed by glaciers, grey and icy, surge around boulders as big as houses and as smooth as river-washed pebbles.

There are only pine trees now, all the tropical and midland traces gone, and tomorrow I will be above the tree line. Yet, in the middle of the trail I encounter a colony of monkeys—macaques, I guess. Living in a little wooded oasis, swinging, chattering and staring at me as I tiptoe by.

There are no communication links unless one climbs up to Jomosom, where there is an outpost of the Nepalese army. We cook over wood fires, and use candles once the sun goes down. One of the marvels I see is a grinding wheel in a little wood house straddling a waterfall. A woman serenely grinds wheat in the middle of a raging 300-foot waterfall. The stone wheel is turned by the paddles hit by the descending water.

At lunch I share my spot in the sun with two sleeping water buffalos. They are such big, lumpy creatures, and chickens are sitting on them as they snore in great rumbles. The bull sounds just like my father. As kids we were so impressed with the noise he could make that we used to go into the bedroom and listen when he took a Sunday nap.

The higher we climb, the more Tibetans pass us on

the trail. Many are barely surviving, and they beg for money or food. Some live in makeshift stone huts that could never keep out the cold nights. These are refugees from the communist Chinese takeover of Tibet . . .

Today begins with a sandstorm. It was so severe last night it blew the tents down. I have never been in the middle of such a bitter, swirling wind. I know the Himalayas test their pilgrims, but what am I doing here, with my shirt tied over my face to keep out the stinging sand? We cross a high plateau bending into a 60 mile-per-hour wind. At times it blows me backward. We finally reach Jomosom, hoping for an oasis and ending up with a dustbowl. A few trekkers gather around a charcoal brazier in a house called the Om Hotel. They are waiting for the small charter plane that can land here. This is the only strip in northwestern Nepal, and the service is unreliable because it is dependent on the wind. They have been waiting four days.

There is only scrub grass at these heights as we move on to Kagbeni, a Tibetan settlement. Yak pastures stretch everywhere. Steep hills and the ever-present, snow-covered Himalayas. I find a faucet in the next village with some warm water heated by a solar panel on the roof. Modern or ancient technology? There has been enough sun that day and I take my first shower in a week.

The Tibetans I meet now still laugh and dance, but they try to sell me silver that is not silver and precious stones that are made of glass. All the stashes they pull out when my white face comes into view are the same. This jewelry is made somewhere else. They know it, I know it, but they are hustling to survive . . .

We continue on through other small settlements. I want to climb higher, to travel in the snow fields, but I have neither the equipment to withstand the cold nor the courage to move any farther from contact with the outside world. When I tumbled down a short cliff today, I realized that a broken bone is a disaster on these high trails. I wanted to climb all the way to Tibet, but the border is still closed and it is below zero tonight. Time to turn around, mark the spot and return to start again.

POTENTIALITY

In every child who is born, under no matter what circumstances, and of no matter what parents, the potentiality of the human race is born again: and in him, too, once more, and of each of us, our terrific responsibility toward life; toward the utmost idea of goodness, of the horror of error, and of God.

—JAMES AGEE,
Let Us Now Praise Famous Men

SOLACE

There is a big increase in the number of people buying teddy bears and other "stuffies." We are looking for solace.

We never outgrow the need for nurturing and support. We like to think there was a magical time when it was ours. A time of innocence.

When mom or dad aren't there, when blankies and squeezies are gone, we try other things. Collecting paintings or cars, trying alcohol or touching, buying comforters helps some. A sense of history helps, too. Doilies are making a comeback. Old photographs of those who have been before seem more important now.

Solace: we find it in many ways. Acknowledge that you need it and deserve it. If you see me having lunch with a bear, smile. We're willing to share.

JOY

I still remember when joy was an elaborate trip somewhere or a wild night of dining, dancing and love. One had to schedule it and get someone else to cooperate. None of us wanted to miss the fire of life.

Yesterday I was sitting on a stump watching chickens scratch for bugs. My son had come over to shingle the chicken house and I was taking the chance to chat. He looked so good. He told me jokes. The chickens went *puck-puck*. The joy was wonderful.

The shift from filet to grubs is a big one. One might at first think the fire has gone out. Yet, I feel it is finally burning closer to the heart.

DESPAIR

*Whenever I find myself growing grim about the mouth;
whenever it is a damp, drizzly November in my soul;
whenever I find myself involuntarily pausing before coffin warehouses, and bringing up the rear of every funeral
I meet; and especially whenever my hypos get such an
upper hand of me, that it requires a strong moral principle to prevent me from deliberately stepping into the
street, and methodically knocking people's hats off—then,
I account it high time to get to sea as soon as I can. This is
my substitute for pistol and ball. With a philosophical
flourish Cato throws himself upon his sword; I quietly
take to the ship.*

—HERMAN MELVILLE,
Moby Dick

Despair stalks us all now and then. It may be personal, philosophical or the condition of the world. What's important is that you have, tucked away in your heart, another path.

When it hits you can sidestep it, attack it, confront it, or run away—but remember—there's an incredible universe right next door.

CIVILIZATION

"I do not think that the measure of a civilization is how tall its buildings of concrete are, but rather how well its people have learned to relate to their environment and fellow man."

—SUN BEAR OF THE CHIPPEWA TRIBE

We are much better at purchasing and storing goods than we are at sharing and disposing of them. We are familiar with recycling, buying goods second-hand, composting, attending swap meets, and other possibilities. Yet, the efforts involved seem too much. The words "quality of life" and "garbage disposal" are rarely spoken in the same breath. Try a shift in perspective.

You can tell how civilized a person is by what he throws away.

ENVY

I keep running heart-first into envy, into people who think that you've got something they don't have. We don't envy just things, we envy feelings. We compare our happiness to the happiness we sense in others.

Comparison of your life with someone else's never provides an answer or satisfaction. Finding something wrong with them only makes us feel better until we run into someone new to envy.

Emotional and material competitions are small death wishes. They reveal a sense of failure and a desire that others share your pain. You can win only by having your own standard. Try to avoid comparison to others. Listen to your own rhythm. Measure happiness by your own heartbeat.

Don't give your life to the successes of others. Keep it for yourself.

AN EXPLORATION

The human heart can go to the length of God.
Dark and cold we may be, but this
Is no winter now. The frozen misery
Of centuries breaks, cracks, begins to move,
The thunder is the thunder of the floes,
The thaw, the flood, the upstart Spring.
Thank God our time is now when wrong
Comes up to face us everywhere,
Never to leave us till we take
The longest stride of soul men ever took.
Affairs are now soul size
The enterprise
Is exploration into God.

—Christopher Fry
(from "A Sleep of Prisoners")

THE ASHES

You must teach your children that the ground beneath their feet is the ashes of your grandfathers. So that they will respect the land, tell your children that the earth is rich with the lives of our kin.

Teach your children what we have taught our children, that the earth is our mother.

Whatever befalls the earth befalls the sons of the earth. If men spit upon the ground, they spit upon themselves.

This we know: the earth does not belong to man; man belongs to the earth. This we know.

All things are connected like the blood which unites one family. All things are connected.

Whatever befalls the earth befalls the sons of the earth. Man did not weave the web of life: he is merely a strand in it. Whatever he does to the web, he does to himself.

Even the white man, whose God walks and talks with him as friend to friend, cannot be exempt from the common destiny.

We may be brothers after all.

We shall see.

One thing we know, which the white man may one day discover — our God is the same God.

You may think now that you own Him as you wish to own our land; but you cannot. He is the God of man, and His compassion is equal for the red man and the white.

This earth is precious to Him, and to harm the earth is to heap contempt on its Creator. . . .

Where is the thicket? Gone.
Where is the eagle? Gone.
The end of living and the beginning of survival.

—CHIEF SEATTLE,
1854

It is a new season with all its life, beauty and passion. Walk through your world gently, breathe deeply, accept the gift of another day.

MULTIPLES

There is more ambivalence in our lives now than there was in the past. There is more confusion and questions of meaning.

In part it is because we live in a multiple-option world. Once we pass basic survival, the options for Americans seem endless. Whether it's choosing a brand and flavor of ice cream, who to live with, or what to believe in.

For those of us raised on Neapolitan and marriage, it's intimidating. Don't try to buy a stereo or a car without a sixteen-year-old to provide advice. There are too many alternatives and variations.

The down side is that life is more complex and decisions wear us out. The up side is that the choices are now ours. We are more tolerant of others who choose differently. We accept a wider spectrum of love, faith, and style.

There is more individual responsibility for what we are and the way we touch our community.

The next time you feel overwhelmed, breathe the freedom in deeply, accept the responsibility, and remember the joy that can go with it. You have the ability to make a unique, individual choice. If it is good, it is yours—if not, you can choose differently next time.

THE LITTLE BIT OF LIFE

The central cause of society's violence and depression stems from each generation's willingness to humiliate its children, both physically and psychologically. They grow up and turn their pain inward on themselves, outward on society—and on subsequent generations.

We want to believe this isn't true. We even pretend to be unaware or deny our own experiences as children or with our children.

It is true. It deeply hurts you and those you love. We carry it inside.

the god of my childhood wears black robes, has horns on his head and carries an ax in his hand. how in the world was I still able to slip past him?
all of my life I have been creeping stealthily through my landscape, under my arm the little bit of life I keep thinking I have stolen.

—MARIELLA MEHR,
Steinzeit (Stone Age)

What can you do with the bit of life you have managed to carry with you? You can stretch it a hundred-fold by lighting the way for children—yours, mine and the child within.

130

ACKNOWLEDGING OTHERS

I'm a fan of recognition, of little acknowledgements of excellence. The possibilities are all around us: a friend who has style, a waitress who smiles, a motorist who allows us in, a co-worker who helps out, a technician who cares, a child who tries.

Excellence is there, it needs only awareness, your attention to expand. You can improve our lives and warm our hearts just by acknowledging a skill or personal attribute. Just by caring.

Rejection hurts — attention heals.

BREAK THE PATTERNS

The passing of bad family patterns through generations is frustrating. We think we are our own person and suddenly realize we're just carrying forth a variation on a theme.

You were preferred by your mother, who made your father feel left out. So now you exclude your husband and prefer your own daughter. Safety resides in repeating a familiar defense system.

Your mother was always disloyal, so you select friends who are disloyal. You go over and over the pain you felt as a child.

Your stepson is seven. Your husband is a wonderful father to him. Yet you want to reject the child because your father didn't have time for you.

The patterns will come up again and again in your life so you have the opportunity to break them.

Love brings up anything unlike itself for the purpose of release.

—SONDRA RAY

AFTER THE ZENITH

"Zenith" describes the expansion of greatness to its fullest: the longest day of the year, the endless summer, the heights of personal success.

Zenith is by its nature brief. The longest day is only one day. Then contraction begins, the cyclic changes continue.

Allow yourself to expect the changes, the rhythm and harmony of your life. Don't waste energy trying to preserve or remember the last zenith.

Stay with the present; it will sustain you through the next decline and shift. Hold within you the knowledge that the ups and downs are always overshadowed by the endurance of love.

MEMORIES

*I am convinced that the greatest legacy we can leave . . .
[is] happy memories: those precious moments so much
like pebbles on the beach that are plucked from the white
sand . . . [then] placed in tiny boxes that lay undisturbed
on tall shelves, until one day they spill out and time
repeats itself, with joy and sweet sadness.*

—OG MANDINO

All of our relationships are forever touched by memories: familiar rituals, moments of understanding, songs, silly ways of talking, family traditions, just being together.

There are so many memories that can be created every day. Which ones are you keeping with you? What memories are you leaving for others?

WHAT PASSION REQUIRES

Passion is a universal life-force. You can breathe it in on cool nights and bright mornings. You can feel it flowing through your body as a ripple of remembered pleasure.

Passion is energy, subtle, variable, and as pure as the life moving through you. It is the secret of self-discipline. Passion requires sustained attention. To achieve its intensity you must sacrifice scope. That is hard for those who skate on the surface, wanting it all.

Open your eyes, open your mind, open your heart, breathe, go deeper, tap into the light.

NEPAL JOURNEY VII

I don't want to turn my back on the mountains. I have been captured. Winding down, the trail is peaceful, familiar. Accustomed to the exertion, the food, and the floors we sleep on, I feel at ease. My guide, always quiet, becomes a shadow, and I slip into my own thoughts.

The path down to Pokhara starts to change me, as I realize I am going toward home, not away from it. I slowly shift from adventurer to traveler, concerned about time and arriving on a day when it will be possible to fly to Katmandu. We cross the last valley into Pokhara, through the bazaar, across the lake on the raft and I say goodbye to Minma, the Sherpa guide, and give him all the equipment and clothes I no longer need. I brought too much and there is no need to carry it back. We have hardly spoken, so have not become friends, only traveling companions . . .

Hot shower, sheets on the bed, dessert and a ride the next morning in a land rover to the airport. A beautiful mountain flight to Katmandu. The reality of baggage, tickets, Katmandu, dirt and too many people who must spend their lives in the streets.

Katmandu is sunk in the fog when I awake, but my flight to Bangkok is on time. Up through the clouds for a last glimpse of the Himalayas through the window. My neck aches from craning to see the last tooth of the jagged, incredible saw across the top of the world.

The sun at this altitude looks like a pale moon, and I start thinking about home. It has been five weeks and a world away from American culture and my family. The altitude and the climb have had little effect on me. The perception of being on top of the world has. I am left with a sense of responsibility because of the options I have that others do not. It is time for a practical commitment to the rest of the world, not a philosophical one.

At the top of the world the issues of survival have little to do with questions of happiness or meaning. I can visit and thrill at the beauty of Nepal, but I return to the security and lifestyle of Seattle.

I find I'm leaving bits and pieces of myself wherever I travel. So much of me will remain in these mountains that I sense I will return soon, to climb the rest of the trail to Tibet, and to reclaim this feeling and these memories . . .

JEALOUSY

Jealousy is, simply and clearly, the fear that you do not have value and that therefore nothing is safe.

Jealousy scans like a beacon, searching for evidence to prove that point—that others will be preferred and rewarded over you.

Jealousy can be a burning pain, as a particular lover chooses another, or a dull, lifelong ache of comparison to everything and everyone.

There is only one alternative—self-value. If you cannot love yourself, you will not believe you are loved. You will always think it's a mistake or blind luck. Take your eyes off others and turn the scanner within. Find the seeds of your jealousy, clear the old voices and experiences. Put all the energy into building your personal and emotional security.

Then you will be the one others envy and you can remember the pain and reach out to them.

THE "LOVE" TEST

Americans are becoming celibate. The love test has gotten impossible to pass. Women told advice-columnist Ann Landers they'd rather hug. Men in reply told Mike Royko they'd rather go bowling. Help!

She: If he comes home on time, is in a good mood and compliments me . . . maybe tonight's the night.

He: If she's combed her hair and cleaned up the kitchen and isn't tired . . . maybe tonight's the night.

She: Well, he passed the first part. Now if he helps with dinner, is nice to the kids, feeds the dog and doesn't turn on TV . . . tonight's the night.

He: If she goes upstairs early, doesn't bring any negatives and brushed her teeth . . .

She: We made it to bed. Well, if the telephone doesn't ring, the kids are quiet . . .

He: If she doesn't blow in my ear and my arm doesn't go to sleep . . .

Argh! Who can pass the great American Let's-Make-Love Test? Don't set up barriers. Enjoy each other. Things will never be perfect, or even close, but it can still be wonderful.

QUIET TIME

Give yourself transition time at the end of the formal work day. It's too hard to shift abruptly from one sphere to the next. You leave part of yourself behind.

There are lots of ways to make the transition, to take off the mask you put on when you went out the door this morning.

Sit in your office and review the day before you end up in a traffic jam. Pull into a park, or to the side of the road, and watch the sky change light. Go for a walk before you enter your home.

You can also make the shift when you get home. Take care of the crises, if there are any, then find a quiet place to sit, read the newspaper, or sweep the front sidewalk. Give yourself at least a few minutes. Make a contract with whomever you live with for "transition time."

Take time to make peace with your day and to renew your energy for the home and people you love.

NEW YEAR

I've just returned from five weeks away, most of it spent trekking in the Himalayas with a guide.

There was no great spiritual breakthrough. I learned that my body is strong, that simplicity is a form of peace, the joy of solitude, and the incredible beauty of the top of the world.

I met people who live very close to the earth and the living things around them. Some nights I slept near chickens and water buffalos. The stars were so close and so bright I felt I could touch them.

I learned the pleasure of climbing up mountains carrying one's home, traveling light, feeling the energy, the freedom, the exhilaration.

I kept a promise that I made at the beginning of last year: to go to Nepal. I now know I will return someday to climb higher and farther.

But now the year is slipping away, and this is the time to think about the promise of the new year, not just the pleasures of the old.

What is your agenda for the new year?

Stop a moment and think about the possibilities that stretch before you.

My agenda was formed in the high country, but it is hard to articulate.

Robert Pirsig has also traveled in mountains, and he writes in *Zen and the Art of Motorcycle Maintenance* more clearly what I am trying to form as a resolution:

I want to talk about another high country now in the world of thought . . . the high country of the mind . . .

Few people travel here. There's no real profit to be made from wandering through it, yet like this high country of the material world around us, it has its own austere beauty that to some people makes the hardships of travel through it worthwhile.

In the high country of the mind, one has to become adjusted to the thinner air of uncertainty . . .

It's time for me to stay closer to home, take risks, write about more private journeys and give on a more practical level. Working on hunger and basic medical care brings one closer to the earth than philosophical questions about meaning. Sharing food and shelter with Nepalese and Tibetans changes priorities.

There is a balance between survival and philosophy. As Peter Matthiessen writes in *The Snow Leopard*, the great sins according to the Sherpas are to pick wildflowers and to threaten children.

It's time to escape the public presence and measure the choices within my own lifespan. It's time that I learned to be mortal.

Mortality is all around us as we recapitulate the events of another year and buy new calendars. We avoid thinking about how many new years we have left.

Listening to the recapitulation of important deaths in the last year, we miss the rebirth promised with the acceptance of our own death. The acceptance of mortality that makes life more precious.

How much time do you have left? And how do you want to spend it?

For the new year, draw a time line on a piece of paper. Put the year of your birth on one end, then each year until 2000. Choose a hypothetical year of death.

- What do you have time for?

- What do you want to stop wasting time on?

- What would you do if you only had a year?

Learn to be mortal as a guide for your life. Weigh your choices against the clock. What are your priorities? What is truly important? What do you want? Do you have time to be abusive or to be abused? What do you have time to care about or give to yourself and your world?

Learning to be mortal is our guide for living.

"Every moment of life is to be lived calmly, mindfully, as if it were the last, to ensure that the most is made of the precious human state," Matthiessen writes in *The Snow Leopard*.

We are all in this life together. What you choose affects us all.

NAMASTE

Along all the paths I traveled these past weeks, I was greeted, even by small children, with hands together as in prayer, head gently bowed and the word "namaste." The greeting translates as "I salute the God within you."

Namaste—friends, readers, travelers: Remember the Spirit within you and between us as another year unfolds. *Remember to take good care of yourself.*

Acknowledgments

The author and publisher gratefully acknowledge Pantheon Books, a division of Random House, Inc., for their kind permission to reprint two paragraphs from *Gift From the Sea*, © Anne Morrow Lindbergh.

Quotation from Alene Moris reprinted by kind permission of Ms. Moris.

Permission to reprint "Abraham Lincoln Walks at Midnight," (from *Collected Poems of Vachel Lindsay*) © 1914 by Vachel Lindsay, renewed 1942 by Elizabeth C. Lindsay, from Macmillan Publishing Company.

About the author

Jennifer James, Ph.D., had been a full-time member of the University of Washington psychiatry department for twelve years when she left, in 1980, to pursue a career in community service and communications. The holder of a doctorate in cultural anthropology and of master's degrees in both history and psychology, she has written a weekly column for the Seattle *Times* for more than seven years. She has written five books, including *Success is the Quality of Your Journey*, which has sold over 100,000 copies. James lectures regularly at schools, universities, and corporations, and also serves as advisor to the Seattle Institute for Child Advocacy and the Community Service Committee.

Share Jennifer James with a friend.

Jennifer James has helped thousands to change their attitudes from the conventional yardsticks of success—and to lead happier, more peace-filled lives. Reward a friend with her writings, or spoken words, on how to stop the grind and share moments of pleasure and warmth.

Success is the Quality of Your Journey: 120 insights and ideas on subjects such as risk, solitude, ageing, and relationships. Over 75,000 copies sold! Trade paperback, 144 pages. (Also available as a 50-minute audio tape, read by the author.)

Windows: 120 more essays on the topics of day-to-day living, intimacy, heroic acts, traveling (including the author's journey to Nepal), and more. Hardcover gift edition and trade paperback, 160 pages.

Ask for these titles at your local bookstore, or order by mail today.

Use this coupon, or write to:
Newmarket Press, 18 East 48th Street, New York, N.Y. 10017

Please send me:

_____ copies of SUCCESS, in paperback @ $8.95 each;
_____ copies of SUCCESS, in audio-cassette form, @ $8.95 each;
_____ copies of WINDOWS, in a hardcover gift edition,
         @ $16.95 each;
_____ copies of WINDOWS, in paperback @ $8.95 each.

Please include applicable sales tax, and add $1.50 for postage and handling (plus 75¢ for each additional item ordered)—check or money order only. Please allow 4-6 weeks for delivery.

I enclose check or money order, payable to Newmarket Press, in the amount of $_____.

Name _____

Address _____

City/State/Zip _____

Clubs, professional groups and other organizations may qualify for special terms on quantity purchases of these titles. For more information, please phone or write: Special Sales Department, Newmarket Press, 18 East 48th Street, New York, N.Y. 10017 (212) 832-3575.

WIN001